THE CHANGING

The Bartons

Audrey Martin

for
The Bartons History Group

Robert Boyd
PUBLICATIONS

Published by
Robert Boyd Publications
260 Colwell Drive
Witney, Oxfordshire OX8 7LW

First published 1999

Copyright © Audrey Martin and
Robert Boyd Publications

ISBN: 1 899536 39 6

TITLES IN THE *CHANGING FACES* SERIES

Banbury: Book One
The Bartons
Bicester: Book One *and* Book Two
Bladon with Church Hanborough and
    Long Hanborough
Botley and North Hinksey: Book One
    and Book Two
St Clements and East Oxford:
    Book One *and* Book Two
Cowley: Book One *and* Book Two *and*
    Book Three
Cowley Works: Book One
Chipping Norton: Book One
Cumnor and Farmoor with Appleton
    and Eaton
St Ebbes and St Thomas: Book One
    and Book Two
Eynsham: Book One *and* Book Two
Faringdon and District
Grimsbury
Headington: Book One *and* Book Two
Iffley
Jericho: Book One *and* Book Two
Kennington
Littlemore and Sandford

Marston: Book One *and* Book Two
North Oxford: Book One *and* Book Two
Oxford City Centre: Book One
South Oxford: Book One *and* Book Two
Summertown and Cutteslowe
West Oxford
Witney: Book One
Wolvercote with Wytham and Godstow
Woodstock: Book One *and* Book Two
Yarnton with Cassington and Begbroke

FORTHCOMING

Abingdon
Banbury: Book Two
Blackbird Leys
Charlbury
Cowley Works: Book Two
Easington
Florence Park
Grimsbury: Book Two
Littlemore and Sandford: Book Two
Oxford City Centre: Book Two
Rose Hill
Thame
Witney: Book Two

Printed and bound in Great Britain at The Alden Press, Oxford

Contents

Front cover photograph

The Bartons Women's Institute egg collection, 1974 (by permission of Leamington Spa Courier) when 600 eggs were collected. Joan Irons is standing in the doorway of Holliers Farm. Down the steps are Joan Sullivan, Isabel Cochran-Wilson, Mary Page and Margaret Cox. Lorraine Greif and Jonathan Green are holding the basket. The collection of eggs to be sent to hospitals each Easter began in The Bartons in 1920, was taken over by the WI and continued until 1977.

Back cover photograph

The ambulance belonging to The Bartons Division of the St John Ambulance Brigade at the County Show at Kidlington Airport in 1948 (by permission of Newsquest (Oxfordshire) Ltd). From left to right: St John Ambulance official, Hilarie Hope (now Bassett), Ada Stockford, and Stan Allington who has described the ambulance *'It was a vehicle without synchromesh gears, without power brakes and with no heating or screen defrosting.'*

Acknowledgements

The Bartons History Group was formed in 1985 and material used in this book has been collected over the years since then. The book, however, could not have been produced without help from many people but some who gave help, and who are named below, have now died. This emphasises the need to record memories of the past before it is too late.

I am grateful to staff at Oxfordshire County Council's Centre for Oxfordshire Studies and at Oxfordshire Archives, and particularly the Oxfordshire County Council Photographic Archive (acknowledged in the text as OPA). Also to the Bodleian Library Oxford, Newsquest (Oxfordshire) Ltd, Banbury Guardian, Leamington Spa Courier, Ordnance Survey, Kelly's Directories Ltd, Hodder & Stoughton and Oxford University Press. I am grateful also to organisations in the village, to Sandford St Martin Cricket Club and to many individuals. All have been generous with their help.

The following people have given permission to use their photographs and drawings or quote from their memories of the past. Many have also provided information, and given invaluable help with the text. Mr David Allen, Mrs Margaret Allen, Mr Stanley Allington, Mr and Mrs Harry and Hilarie (née Hope) Bassett, Mr Kenneth Bauckham, Mr Rodney Benfield, Mr Graham Bradshaw, Mrs Doris Bricknell (née Baker), Mrs Mandy Burrup (formerly Hughes), Mrs Madge Byford, Mr Kenneth Castle, Mrs Barbara Clark, Mr John Cooper, Mr Jim Coster, Mrs Lettie Cross (née Hawkins), Mr Charles Eaglestone, Mr Roy Eaglestone, Mr Robin Fleming, Mr Frank Gascoigne, Mrs Winifred Gibbons (née Gooding), Mr Denis Gibson, Mrs Ann Gross, Mr Colin Harrington, Mr Charles Hazell, Mrs Gladys Hudson (née Houghton), Mr Bill Irons, Mr Jack Irons, Mr Derrick Jarvis, Mr Kenneth Jeffries, Miss Ruth Kirby, Mrs Cynthia Laws, Mrs Jean Luing-Crozier, Mr Malcolm Luing, Mrs Brenda Lydiatt (née Rogers), Mr John Madden, Mrs Kathleen Mandeman (née Saich), Miss Elsie Matthews, Mrs and Mrs Norman and Brenda (née White) Monk, Mrs June Morgan, Mr James Moulder, Mrs Kathleen Murray, Mrs Jean Nippress (née Dallinger), Mrs Lucy Norton, Mrs Mona Owen (née Kirby), Mrs Mary Page, Miss Heather Perren, Mrs Marion Pettengell (née Hazell), Mrs Kathleen Phillips, Mr Eric Pratley, Mrs Monica (Bubbles) Pratley (née Stockford), Mrs Ruby Pratley, Mr Percy Prior, Mr Tony Probitts, Mr and Mrs Tony and Julia (née Hope) Reed, Mrs Rowland, Mr John Simson, Mr Jack Smith, Miss Kay Stewart, Mrs Margaret Stewart, Miss Joan Sullivan, Mr Peter Watts, Mr Ronald Webb, Miss Celia Wannan, Mr Peter Winchester. Every effort has been made to trace ownership of material used in this book, and I apologise if proper acknowledgement is not made. Invaluable help in making copies of photographs has been given by Rodney Munday, Devril Page and, with assistance in other ways as well, by members of my family.

Very many people have given information — a complete list would exceed the space available. I can only express my great gratitude to all who have been so willing to share their memories, and to all who have helped with the publication of this book.

Preface

Village life in The Bartons now is very different from that in the first half of the century. The village nurse then helped to bring people into the world and the village undertaker made the coffin and arranged the funeral when they died. Most people worked in the village or at farms and large houses in the surrounding area and the local blacksmith and harness maker repaired the farm machinery. Children could play in the road or roam the fields and wild flowers were plentiful. Corn was ground at the mill, there were several shops and most of the entertainment was within the village. The Bartons, too, had a strong tradition of independence and Nonconformity and had their own Friendly Society to provide insurance against the costs of burial and ill health. It was a mainly self-supporting community still remembered by the older generation.

The aim of this book is to present a record of some aspects of that self-supporting community by using photographs, with brief comments enlivened, where possible, by personal memories.

Most of the photographs are of people because it is the people and the village families, many with descendants still living here today, who have played such an important part in shaping the history. This is not a complete account of that history. Many events and many people are not mentioned, for there is not space enough to include all the material we have. There are also gaps in this material so any further photographs or memories will always be welcomed.

It is hoped that the book will give pleasure to those who regard The Bartons with affection as something special, and that it will be of interest to all who would like to know more about them.

LOCAL BOOKLETS

Available from The Bartons History Group, 11 Enstone Road, Middle Barton, Oxon, OX7 7BL.

Bartons History Group publications
Barton Abbey, revised 1996.
The History of the Bartons, G Laws, 1985.
Middle Barton. A Village Walk, 1988.
Middle Barton School. Aspects of School Life 1866–1996, Audrey Martin, 1997.
The Parish Church, Steeple Barton, 1993.
Westcote Barton Parochial Church Council
The Parish Church, Westcote Barton, 1993.
The Bartons Women's Institute
It Happened in the Dorn Valley 1939–1945, 1945, reprinted 1987.

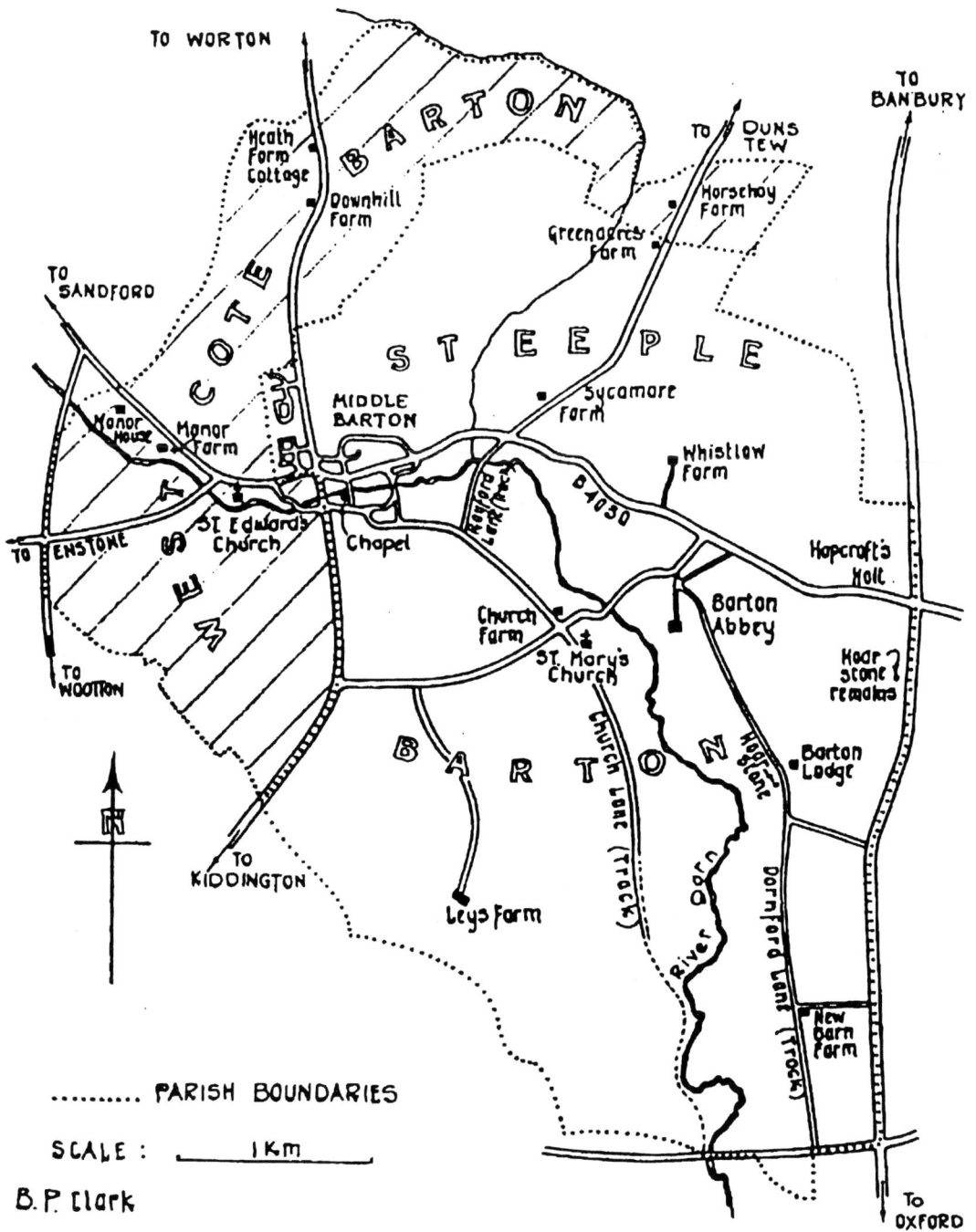

TO WORTON

TO BANBURY

C O T E   B A R T O N

Heath Farm Cottage

Downhill Farm

TO DUNS TEW

Horschay Farm

Greenacres Farm

TO SANDFORD

S T E E P L E

MIDDLE BARTON

Sycamore Farm

Whistlow Farm

Manor House

Manor Farm

B4030

Hopcroft's Holt

TO ENSTONE

St Edwards Church

Chapel

Raford Lane (track)

Barton Abbey

Hoar Stone remains

S T E E P L E

Church Farm

St Mary's Church

Barton Lodge

TO WOOTTON

B A R T O N

Hogg Lane

River Dorn

Dornford Lane (track)

New Barn Farm

TO KIDDINGTON

Leys Farm

Church Lane (track)

TO OXFORD

.... PARISH BOUNDARIES

SCALE : _____ 1 Km

B. P. Clark

N

Map of The Bartons, 1990s. Maps are based upon Ordnance Survey 1:25 000 scale mapping with the permission of The Controller of Her Majesty's Stationery Office © Crown copyright.

Introduction

The Bartons are in North Oxfordshire, half way between Oxford and Banbury, and some explanation of the name is needed. There are two parishes, Steeple Barton and Westcote Barton with their parish churches in the 'hamlets' of Steeple Barton to the east and Westcote Barton to the west of the area. These are old settlements. Steeple Barton has hoar stones and Neolithic finds going back 5000 years, and Westcote Barton has a church where Saxon stone foundations have been discovered.

Middle Barton, with a Methodist chapel, is in the centre, and although historically part of Steeple Barton parish, the name is now often used to describe a central area cutting across parish boundaries. There is often, understandably, confusion. The term Middle Barton is used in this book in its modern sense to describe this central part where most of the people live. Present day street names and house numbers were not introduced until the late 1960s. They are, however, used in this book to identify buildings.

The name Barton indicates an outlying farm and it is believed that corn was sent from Steeple Barton in Saxon times to the royal court at Woodstock, and then later to Oseney Abbey. In medieval times there was a sizeable settlement near the church, but after that, most of the population moved away — the land was wanted for sheep, new trading routes were opening up, population was decimated by the Black Death, and, some 600 years ago, people moved west to form a new centre, and Middle Barton came into being. The Bartons remained relatively unchanged until the early 19th century when, as a result of enclosure, land was allotted to new (mainly absentee) landowners and new farms and houses were built.

During the 19th century there was an influx of settlers into the 'open village' of Middle Barton. Land was not under the control of just one or two owners, as in some neighbouring villages, and many trades people and workers came to build houses and to rent cottages or find work on local farms. There was also another 19th century development which affected the history of The Bartons. Two Victorian families bought land and property. The Revd Jenner Marshall (not the incumbent) had his manor house built in Westcote Barton. The Hall family, of the Oxford Brewery, built up their estate centred on the house they named Barton Abbey in Steeple Barton.

By the mid-20th century both estates had been sold, and it was the re-sale of Hall land in Middle Barton that made possible the housing developments of the 1960s and 1970s. Yet more people moved into Middle Barton to occupy these new houses, and the population, which had steadily been declining, increased. As a result the village can still support some services and, what is very important, a thriving village primary school.

Sketch maps of the central part of the village

1790s

The Enclosure Award of 1796 gave land, previously farmed in the open field system, to new owners. The Enclosure Award map, as well as showing the newly enclosed fields, also showed roads and buildings. There were then only two on the north side of the main road.

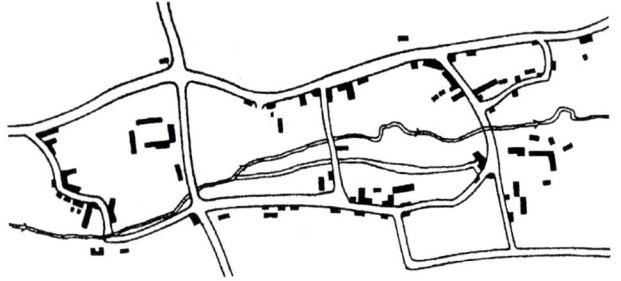

1880s

By 1881, houses had been built on the roadside waste along the main road and on the road leading to Worton. Many of the older houses had been divided into small cottages.

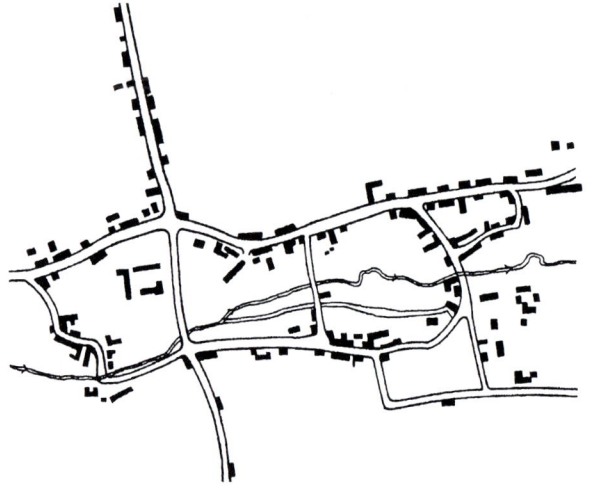

1990s

In the second half of the 20th century, many of the houses divided up into cottages were turned again into larger homes. New houses were built, and the present day map gives a clear picture of the development that has taken place throughout the village and particularly on the north side.

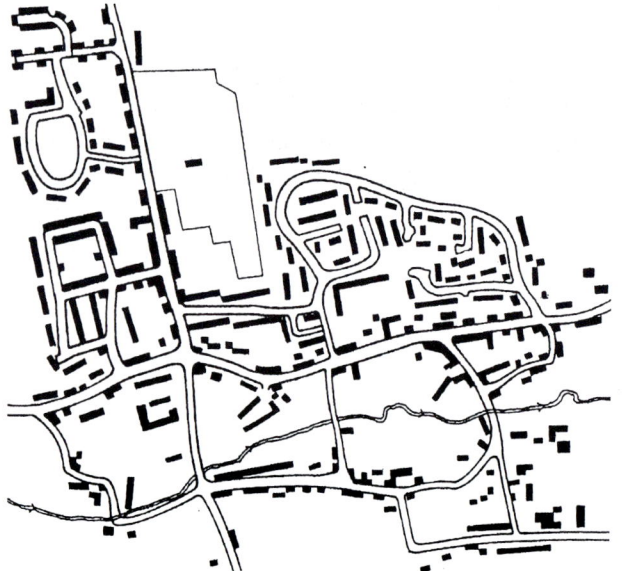

Middle Barton

Most of the people live in Middle Barton and the book begins with a tour of that area, including some of the village shops and services.

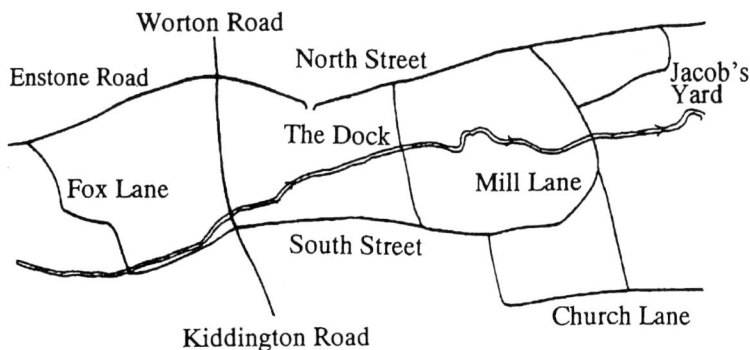

Worton Road

Enstone Road

North Street

Jacob's Yard

The Dock

Fox Lane

Mill Lane

South Street

Church Lane

Kiddington Road

MIDDLE BARTON
— FROM THE KIDDINGTON ROAD —

A view of the village from the south c1920 (OPA), taken from Kiddington Road, later known locally as Hard Road Hill, the first road here to be given such a surface. The picture shows a cottage in the foreground, now gone. It shows the six houses of Washington Terrace in the centre of the picture with a path by the houses and washing hanging in their gardens the other side of the path. The gardens were well tended and many family groups used to take a Sunday afternoon walk along this path. People were living in Washington Terrace until 1978 but the houses were demolished in 1993 and have now been replaced by a modern building development. The footpath by those houses led to the main road, now called North Street, where the buildings covered with creeper housed a shop and the shopkeeper's family. There were then only fields beyond.

North Street

This photograph, c1900, is a closer view of the creeper-covered house and shop on the main road. The picture, looking towards the Worton/Kiddington crossroads, shows an area that is now greatly changed. The three cottages on the left have been pulled down and replaced by a new housing development. The picture also shows two of the eight village shops. On the right there was the shop run by the Luing family. On the other side of the road, beyond the three cottages on the left, was a butcher's shop belonging to Charles John Eaglestone. The brick butcher's shop had not yet been built.

This photograph was taken when Charles John Eaglestone and Elizabeth Miriam Woodward were married in 1890. She came from a butcher's family in Woodstock and helped her husband run the shop. A son was born, but two years later Elizabeth died in child-birth. Charles Eaglestone then sold the business and left the village.

There are, however, still three generations of the Eaglestone family living in Middle Barton today, descendants of Eaglestones (the name is spelt in many different ways) who have lived in the village since at least 1642. Members of the family, who have been researching their history, combined with The Bartons History Group in 1995 to organise a reunion. Descendants of Barton Eaglestones and relations came from as far afield as Yorkshire, Bristol and Ireland.

Thomas Grace Barrett standing in the doorway of the shop he bought in 1903 from Charles Eaglestone. He bought the row of four cottages for £450 and paid £10 for the shop fittings. Soon afterwards, he had a new shop built next door.

Stan Gardner outside this shop, shortly before it closed in 1988.

The shop and house opposite the butcher's was built in the mid-19th century by William Luing, great-great-grandson of the first William Luing in the village. The shop, a general stores, was run by members of the family for the next fifty years, by which time two of the daughters, Lydia and Susannah, had turned it into a draper's. Photographs, taken c1860, of William and Mary Ann Luing and seven of their ten children have been kept by Mona Owen, née Kirby, a descendant of the family.

William Luing, father.

William's daughter Martha, Mona's grandmother.

William's son, also William.

Son William set up a business on the opposite side of the road from the shop. He was a clothier and legging maker, though a bill-head indicates that he turned his hand to many other things as well.

BARTON CLOTHING AND SHOE WAREHOUSE,

4 May _____ 186*0*

Mr C Nichols

Bought of W. LUING, JUN.,

WOOLLEN DRAPER, TAILOR, CLOTHIER, BOOT AND SHOE MANUFACTURER,
PRINTER, BOOKBINDER, AND BOOK AND NEWS AGENT.

The area was a hub of commercial activity. A warehouse was built, a shoemaker's workshop adjoined 16 North Street, and some of the workers lived in Washington Terrace. The business grew into quite a large scale industry, and William Luing also had a shop in Banbury. He is described in the 1871 census as a master clothier employing 7 men, 7 women and 1 boy, but by 1880 the business was bankrupt.

This area, however, continued to be a site of commercial activity. The warehouse, the two-storey part of No. 20, housed a plumber's business for a time. After that, Walter Howe developed his haulage and coal business. There were family connections in the businesses here. Walter Howe married a daughter of Thomas Barrett, the butcher further along the road. Another of Thomas Barrett's daughters married Ralph Prior and their son Percy, after the Second World War, started his own haulage business which he carried on here until he moved away in 1988.

On the other side of the road, the shop, now Kirby & Co, was once again a general stores being run by Phil and Marianne Kirby, who were relatives of the Luings — Marianne was Martha's daughter. Their daughters, Winnie and Mona, worked in the shop helped by their cousin Ruth Kirby who has written about her time there.

'We started at 8 o'clock and worked until 7 at night, 9 o'clock on Saturdays. We used to weigh up all the goods, sugar, lard, cheese, etc. and cut up large blocks of salt. In addition my cousins and I took it in turns to go and get orders covering a very wide area on bicycles. We travelled round Sandford, Ledwell and the Wortons one week and Gagingwell, Radford and Kiddington the next. We also covered the village, Barton Abbey and Barton Lodge. The goods were delivered first by horse and cart and later by van.'

The post in the foreground was one of the oil street lights provided by Steeple Barton Parish Council in 1898. Six of them, stormproof and thirty candle power, were added to two already in existence at a cost of £1 10s per light. William Stewart was paid £9 4s a year to maintain and light them within one hour of sunset to 10.15pm. A resident asked if the light by her house on the main road could be removed as *'children and others congregated and made a disturbance'*. The parish council agreed to move the lamp. In 1907, however, the street lighting was discontinued because it was too expensive. Street lights were put in again, powered by electricity this time, in 1954. The photograph is one of a series of pictures of the village taken, in about 1920, for Kirby & Co. People who moved here forty years later were delighted to find that the photographs were still available. A mistake had been made in the number of noughts when they were ordered and thousands instead of hundreds were printed!

The Kirby family gave up the shop in 1933 and it was then bought by Edward Cox.

A 1940s photograph (OPA) shows Mark Stockford senior, with Kitty the mare, delivering bread for Hedley Gardiner senior, who ran the bakery in South Street from the late 1930s to 1946 having taken it over from William Constable. When Edward Cox's son Ewart retired in 1977 the shop closed and the property was sold. It was later made into three houses, and part is now a children's home. By this time the row of cottages on the other side of the road had become derelict. Two of the buildings had datestones which gave clues to their history. TWC 1908 on a building, later the Prior haulage business office, marked a shop put up by Thomas Claridge in competition with Kirby's. The other was on a house built in 1819 by John Parsons, a carpenter, who owned the row of cottages here. After his death in 1870, they were put up for sale and were advertised as four substantially built and slated cottages with butcher's shop, carpenter's shop and hovels pleasantly situated in the centre of the town.

It is this datestone (drawn by Barbara Clark for the booklet *Middle Barton. A Village Walk*) that is set in the wall at the side of the present day development which replaces the cottages.

The house in the foreground, c1905, is now 34 North Street. Bay windows were fitted soon afterwards and it became a shop belonging to Walter and Gertrude Parsons. He was a builder and she managed the shop. In 1926, Harry Allday took it over. His niece Gladys Houghton helped him and, after he died, ran the shop until 1938. Her note 'Those were the Days' includes the following memories. *'Mr. Humphries, the Carrier, into Banbury every Thursday. What a memory, he just looked at our order and said "I shall remember that" and sure enough he did and never once made a mistake. His means of transport was horse and cart. I remember Harry Golder who dug a hole in the garden once a week, for the 'you know what'. My uncle gave him half an ounce of twist (4d) each week.* (It was 1951 before main drains were installed.) *Shop hours 7 a.m. to 8.30 p.m., 9 p.m. Saturdays. Then deliver groceries on my cycle after these hours. Did I say Those were the Days?*

Part of The Three Horseshoes, one of three pubs, can be seen beyond the house. It had ceased to be a pub by 1933 and the front part was made into an ironmongers shop.

Eric Pratley took it over from Ralph Greenslade in 1965 and his brother Roy and Roy's wife Ann are seen here helping to put up signs. The shop and petrol pumps closed in 1971, and after that the building was demolished and six terraced houses built on the site.

The sign of The Three Horseshoes is seen from the other direction, and on the opposite side of the road was the Post Office, run by the Grimsleys from 1895 to 1933. By 1930, when this picture (OPA) was taken, the telephone had arrived. The Grimsleys were also builders and painters and their workshop adjoined the house, 23 North Street.

Just beyond are four houses built in 1928 for the Rural District Council, which was based then at Woodstock. One of the village standpipes was put outside these houses ten years later when mains water was installed. The Steeple Barton Parish Council suggested that posters should be put up stating that 'the Bartons water is fit to drink'. Not everyone, however, greeted this new system with such approval. A resident is said to have complained that his tea just didn't have the same flavour as when made with water from the brook. Just as, when electricity came in 1933, one lady still used a candle to light herself to bed — *that electric ain't safe'.*

This house, 41 North Street, was known for many years as The Cottage on the Horse Common, a name taken from information in early title deeds that the owner had rights to use the common or open fields at the rear of the house. The building, now gone, between the house and the pavement was used for many purposes, including a library, war time billets for soldiers, tea room, antique dealer,

doctor's surgery, storage for musical instruments, a TV repair workshop.

The house a little further along is called Sam's Hill Cottage, a reminder that the fields behind were used by Sam Simson to break in his horses. Further back in time, from at least 1601, fields to the north were called Barnhill. This name has now been replaced by Holliers named after the family who, for a time, lived at the farm at the junction of North Street and Mill Lane, now known as Holliers Farm and still a farm with animals grazing on land in the centre of the village.

Middle Barton Garage was established in 1923 by Bob Jarvis, son of Thomas Jarvis the saddler. Bob was first of all described as a carrier, but he was soon to set up a business with motor vehicles and before long was given the official title of Motor Omnibus Proprietor. He retired in 1962 and his two sons, Derrick and David, who were partners, carried on the business.

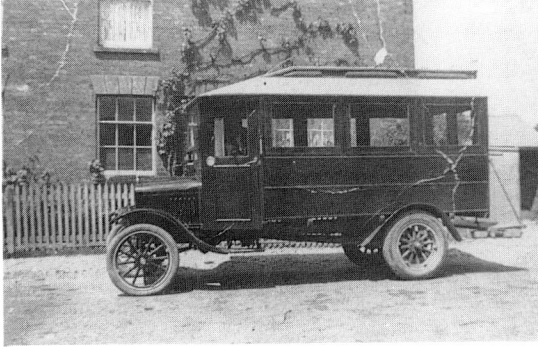

An early coach. The first vehicle was open and when people were travelling in it, benches were put in for them to sit on. By today's standards we would think it very uncomfortable, but the excitement then and the pleasure of a ride in the bus was tremendous. People still talk about it and remember travelling to the Wembley Exhibition in London in 1925.

Drivers of the coaches on a Sunday School outing in about 1950. Left to right: Jack Smith, Harry Stevens, Derrick Jarvis.

Petrol pumps at the garage in 1959, and Carol Jarvis in her Brownie uniform.

By 1972 the garage had been sold to Ronald Winfield, and soon afterwards the coach business to Heyfordian.

The post office moved to George Kirby's house, 67 North Street, when he became Postmaster in 1933. He was a tailor, and is shown in this photograph with his daughter Ruth in 1914. The large window, built to let in light for the tailoring business, was later reduced in size. The post office was underneath the tailoring workshop. Ruth Kirby helped her father, and was later Postmistress herself for 36 years until she retired in 1982. The post office then moved to Webb's shop in Worton Road. George Kirby was a Methodist preacher and his daughter was involved in chapel and other village activities. She gave help in so many different ways that everyone was delighted when she was awarded a BEM and its presentation was a village celebration.

Next door but one, No. 71, used to be the police house — in the 1920s the village had its own policeman — and in 1925 William Franklin was living here.

This picture shows William Franklin at a meet at Barton Abbey.

A 1920s photograph (OPA) shows, on the right, the saddler's shop and his house next to it, 96 North Street, with just beyond it the front of the wooden building which was a cinema.

Harry Bradshaw had been working with Thomas Jarvis at the saddler's and took it over in 1920 after Thomas Jarvis died. He repaired saddles and harness and also repaired shoes. Later on, his son Fred did shoe repairs and had a shoe and knitting wool shop there.

Fred Bradshaw also built a splendid model railway, featured several times on television, which was visited by people from all over the world. Sadly both shop and railway closed in 1982.

Part of the model railway, with many landscape features, which included a roundabout in action and a bonfire which produced smoke, and with day and night sequences.

The cinema in the 1950s. It had started in 1924 in a wooden building, run by Albert Constable and known then as The Premier Cinema, with an engine at the back to provide power. The films were silent in those days but there was sometimes a pianist to provide music. Later on, a more solid building was put up around the wooden structure.

The cinema provided entertainment for people from the surrounding area, and the Jarvis coaches provided transport. The tickets included the cost of the cinema and the cost of the coach. At that time, too, there was a fish and chip shop almost next door, at 110 North Street, which was well supported by the cinema audiences – fish and chips and the drink 'Tizer'.

The cinema was taken over during the war to provide sleeping quarters for the army. After that, the new owner, James Smith, installed up-to-date equipment and the re-named Palace Cinema had the first cinemascope showing in Oxfordshire, as reported in the Oxford papers in October 1954.

CinemaScope has first Oxfordshire showing

THE panoramic screen process of CinemaScope had its first Oxfordshire showing before an invited audience last night at the tiny 206 - seater Palace Cinema, Middle Barton—the smallest cinema in Europe to show it.

There were two new programmes each week until it closed in 1963. The building was used as business premises and offices until it was demolished in 1998 and two houses have now been built on the site.

The photograph, taken in 1959, shows houses in North Street. A car was parked not very far from the garage, and a coach alongside the cinema. The fields to the north of North Street had not yet been built on and the track between Nos. 67 and 69 shows clearly. The house in the foreground to the left is now 6 Jacob's Yard and the house next to it No. 5.

The main road c1920, probably the only time it was called High Street! The three houses on the right were demolished to make way for the road into The Firs estate built in 1980. The house with the alleyway was used by Dr Jones for his surgery. It had the advantage that people could wait under cover in this alleyway. At the other surgery, in the house by the garage, people had to wait outside to see Dr Turner. Note also the heap of stones which would be used for repairing the road. At that time there were two doctors from Deddington who held surgeries in the village. The following information is given in Kelly's Directory for Oxfordshire, 1915.

STEEPLE BARTON.

Dillon Arthur, Barton lodge (letters through Steeple Aston)
Hall Alexander William D.L., J.P. Barton abbey
Stephen Rev. Simon D.D., Ph.D. (vicar), Vicarage

COMMERCIAL.

Goffe Wm. Garner, frmr.Church frm
Harper Robert, farm bailiff to A. W. Hall esq

MIDDLE BARTON.

Hall Miss, Abbey Wood
Haynes Miss

COMMERCIAL.

Baker George, wheelwright
Baker William, carpenter

Barrett Thomas G. butcher
Bronsdon Walter, Carpenters' Arms P.H
Castle Moses, wheelwright
Constable William John, farmer
Farley Harry, beer retailer
Grimsley Elizh. S. (Mrs.), stationer
Grimsley Wm. builder, Post office
Harris Henry, miller (water & steam)
Hope Geo.Fdk. Three Horseshoes P.H
Irons William, builder
Jackman Joseph, blacksmith
Jarvis Thomas, boot dealer
Jones G. Horatio M.R.C.S.Eng., L.R.C.P.Lond. physician & surgeon & certifying factory surgeon; attends from Deddington, mondays, wednesdays & fridays

Jones Richard, blacksmith
Kirby & Co. grocers
Kirby George, tailor
Marsh Charles, builder
Parsons James, shopkeeper
Parsons Walter, shopkeeper
Soden John, nurseryman & florist, Grove nursery
Stockford Susan (Mrs.), shopkeeper
Stockford Tom, shopkeeper
Temperance Hall
Turner Thomas W., M.R.C.S.Eng., L.R.C.P. Lond.physician & surgeon, & medical officer & public vaccinator, No. 1 district, Woodstock union; attends from Deddington, mondays, wednesdays & fridays
Wells William, boot maker

These two doctors visited from the late 1880s to the 1930s. Dr Hodges joined Dr Jones and they are remembered as performing greatly appreciated pantomimes in the villages served by the practice. Proceeds from Little Red Riding Hood here in 1933 were donated to village hall funds, and local talent was recruited – 'Bubbles' Stockford, Cissie Taylor, Winnie and Queenie Shirley and Violet Bolton.

After the war, when Dr Wollaston, Dr McCabe and Dr Watson were doctors from the single practice in Deddington, the surgery was held in the front part, now gone, of 41 North Street where there was a waiting room. The doctors in 1966 moved their surgery to the Alice Marshall Hall where a baby clinic (with helpers from the local Women's Institute) was held regularly, but when the health centre in Deddington was opened in 1974 surgeries and clinic were no longer held in the village.

The area beyond the entrance to The Firs estate used to be covered with the greenhouses and plants of the market garden run by the Soden family from the 1840s until the 1920s. The gardens extended over several acres and the Sodens were successful competitors at horticultural shows in Oxfordshire.

The Carpenters Arms, on the other side of the road, in the 1920s (OPA). It was recorded as Fleur de Luce from 1774, but by 1837 the name had been changed to The Carpenters Arms. It was bought by William Hall, of the Oxford Brewery, in 1823 from Thomas Gould, who lived in the house just beyond the pub, for £800 and £12 for the fixtures. The outside still looks much as it did in the 1920s, but the interior has been modernised and meals are now served.

The Bicester/Enstone road was a turnpike road from 1793 to 1876 and, after that, the Barton toll house and gate were put up for sale. These were at the junction of the main road, the B4030, and Duns Tew Road. It is believed that the people in the picture, c1905, were from the Mole family standing in front of their house.

Fields to the west of the Duns Tew Road have been designated a Site of Special Scientific Interest. This is fen, unusual for this part of Oxfordshire, and a result of the lack of change in the way the land has been farmed. There are also old hedgerows here.

Jacob's Yard

The Kirby family played a large part in village life and this photograph of Jeremiah Kirby with his wife and family is of particular interest as it was taken just three months after the 1891 census when Jeremiah Kirby himself was enumerator. The photograph was taken outside their house, now part of 6 Jacob's Yard, when their son Richard was married to Agnes Connington on the 14th July 1891. Left to right, back row: Annie, Sabina, Maud, George Henry, parents Ann and Jeremiah, Ruth. Front row: Phil, Bessie, Fanny, Agnes and Richard, a relation of the bride?, and Rhoda. George Henry became a tailor and postmaster, and Phil was later to run the village stores.

Details of the family are shown on the last page of the census return for Steeple Barton parish. Ann's father William Finch had married Ann Hollis and these names had been given to the daughters.

The name Mill Street was used in the census and often described part of what is now known as Jacob's Yard. The name Jacob's Yard then applied only to the area near the main road but no information has so far been found to explain why it was so called. In the 19th century, original houses were divided up, and others were built to house the workers who had come to live here. Numbers had dropped by 1891 but there were still 22 households, made up of 53 adults and 28 children aged 14 and under, all living in what we now know as Jacob's Yard. Today there are nine houses. Many Barton people were Nonconformist and Quaker Cottage, 2 Jacob's Yard, was, from 1700 to 1846, used as a Quaker Meeting House; the burial ground opposite the house was, for a short time in the early 18th century, used for Quaker burials.

Mill Lane

Household belongings perhaps being transported in Mill Lane by Tom Jeffries, who was one of the village bakers, in about 1905. The outlet of a spring can be seen beyond the pony's legs, and many people used to fetch water from this spring rather than from the brook. There also used to be cottages here used sometimes in the 1890s for Salvation Army meetings. Mill Lane leads to the main road and part of the building in the background, No. 6, was a shop and off-licence with beer sold through the hole, now bricked up, in the wall of the house. A brick building was put up nearby and became a shop taken over by the Farley family in 1912.

Florrie Farley in the shop in 1977. She had trained as a teacher but after her father's death in 1935, came to help her mother in the shop. She stayed and was still living in 6 Mill Lane and running the shop when she died in 1980. The shop closed then and the house has now been extended to include the brick building.

The Mill

Middle Barton grew up around the mill, almost certainly a Domesday mill recorded in 1086, and a working corn mill up to the beginning of the Second World War.

This photograph in the Kirby series, c1920, shows the steam engine in the yard, used occasionally to supply extra power. The Harris family ground corn at the mill from 1854 to 1920, had a bakery and would also grind the corn people grew on allotments or gleaned after harvesting.

Walter Allen, pictured here in about 1930, was the last miller.

Lilian Davis sitting by the side of the 'sheep wash'. Her father Frederick Charles Allen was one of the family of the last millers and the photograph was taken shortly before the mill closed down. By the side of the mill was the overflow of water from the mill stream where sheep from this, and from other villages, were washed.

'When I was a boy, I saw the sheep being pushed in the water with a long crook. I stood in Mill Lane and kept them confined when they were finished. The farmer Mr Goffe, gave me two pence and said Thank you. Two whole pence, real money, I felt rich.' (Denis Gibson.)

The water came out into Mill Lane, and on the other side of the lane was a small cottage. Now all that remains is a bricked up fireplace in the wall of the drive leading to 7 Mill Lane.

Number 7 Mill Lane is now one house but it used to be two cottages when this photograph was taken, c1950, of George and Henrietta Davis sitting outside the front doors. Lilian Davis was the wife of their son Ernest.

South Street

William John Constable was the farmer at Home Farm, now a house and no longer a farm. Shortly before he died in 1954, when he was 91 and still farming, he looked back into the past and commented: *'In some ways the past was preferable to the present, people were not so self-satisfied then.'* He also had a bakery at the farm. Bread and cakes were baked and on Sundays the aroma of the dinners being cooked used to waft round the village. Very few people had ovens big enough to cook a joint. The men, and it was men only, took the meat on a tray with a jug of Yorkshire pudding mixture, to the bake-house. They returned at 12 o'clock with a tea cloth to take home the cooked meat and Yorkshire pudding. The men also had a social chat!

A Kirby photograph, c1920, shows Home Farm in the foreground on the right. Next door, at No. 45, was the house and smithy where three generations of the Baker family lived and carried on the business of blacksmith and wheelwright.

William Baker c1900 by the smithy at the back of the house.

The orchard on the other side of the road has now been built on. Just beyond is the house where William and Dorothy Pilling had their shop from the 1950s to 1970s. There had also been other shops in South Street.

Clara Hawkins, c1930, standing in the doorway of the shop she kept in the front rooms of the house, No. 44, where she and her husband Jesse lived. Very often it was the wife who managed the shop to make a little extra money to augment the family income.

The bottle over the door advertised the fizzy drink 'monster'.

LYONS TEA 4D PER 1/4 lb

Children used to buy sweets there on the way to school. Some just looked in!

The house below is 33 South Street, in about 1930. It has since been extended but not greatly changed. It is a cruck framed, late medieval house, and is the oldest building in the central part of the village. For many years it was a shop and the small door in the Dock footpath was the door into the shop. George and Susan Stockford lived there in the first part of the 19th century, and she managed the shop. Their son George became organist and choirmaster at Steeple Barton church.

The car, a bullnose Morris, was owned by Charles Boffin and it was parked on the area known as The Green, possibly so called to describe the meeting place for the Chapel camp meetings.

Charles Boffin standing by his car in front of the barn where he kept it. The barn has been converted into rooms, part of 35 South Street; the name of the house is Barn Cottage.

36 South Street, now much enlarged, used to be a small cottage lived in for nearly 20 years, until 1983, by Marjorie Chrystie. The title deeds of her house indicated that it was probably part of a house sold in 1714, in Queen Anne's time, for £14.

A picture in the Kirby series, c1920, looking east up South Street towards the Green.

The single-storey building on the right was a shared wash house. Many tasks then were done by people working together. One lady, however, is remembered as spending long hours in the wash house as she made extra money for the household by taking in washing.

The mill stream was diverted from the brook at a sluice, or lasher, in the field on the other side of the road. Many children used to play here and it was known locally as 'the waterfall'.

1925. Betty and Jean Dallinger, grandchildren of Harry and Bess (née Eaglestone) Hancock, at the 'waterfall'. The stream then flowed under the raised footbridge at The Dock and on to the mill. The channel is now filled in but its route in this field is marked by the boundary line of the back gardens of South Street houses built in the 1960s.

The middle house on the bank behind, 4 South Street, has been much altered but has a datestone which gives the information that it was set upon free land in 1696.

John Carpenter in 1930, using a yoke to carry his buckets, would have been fetching water from the brook. At the nearby bridge, as at the other bridges over the river Dorn, were steps at the side (still there) which led to a 'keaching' stone where people stood to draw their supplies of water.

Fox Lane

Fox Lane ford, in the parish of Westcote Barton, in the 1920s. (OPA) The house on the left is Old Mill Cottage and in the 18th century there was a mill here, said to have been powered from a spring. The house on the right, owned by the Jarvis family for a hundred years until 1900 was, for a few years in the 1980s, the home of the leading Labour politician Bryan Gould.

The ford, one of two in the village, is popular with children in summer time and they come to play and paddle here, and the footbridge over the Dorn is much used for playing 'pooh sticks'.

Within living memory trout and crayfish were plentiful. They disappeared when the brook became polluted. It is clean again and people claim to have seen trout, though not very big ones.

A view looking north c1905. The cottages on the left have been altered. The one nearest the foreground has been demolished and the others beyond it rebuilt.

The history of houses in Fox Lane, like that of Jacob's Yard, reflects the prosperity, or lack of it, of the time. We know that there were some quite sizeable properties here in the 18th century. During the 19th century most of these houses were divided up and other cottages were built. This extract from the Ordnance Survey map 1881 shows the Fox Lane cottages.

The census taken in 1881 gives the information that there were 31 occupied and 9 unoccupied cottages in Fox Lane with 69 adults and 64 under 15-year olds living in these 31 cottages.

Most of the cottages were just one room up and one down with shared privies and a rent of about 1 shilling and 4 pence a week. Many were rented by farm labourers whose wages were not more than ten shillings a week.

By the 1920s the cottages were much less crowded and, in the second half of the 20th century, some cottages were joined together again, some were reconstructed and some new ones built. There are now 15 houses in place of the 40 cottages noted in 1881.

The back view of 17 Fox Lane, the home for many years in the early part of the 20th century, of Fred and Winifred Probitts. The building nearest the ford had been made into two cottages. After that, it became derelict and has recently been incorporated into a new house. A lancet window in the south wall (perhaps built by a local stonemason?) has been retained.

There were 'yards' in Fox Lane, where the doors into the cottages were not directly from the road but where one entrance led to several cottages either arranged around a court yard (Jarvis Yard) or in a row which backed on to the road (Savery's Yard). These were named after owners, and the name Chapel Yard was sometimes used as one of the houses, part of No. 10, had originally been built as a Primitive Methodist chapel.

Two of the Jarvis Yard cottages in the 1930s. The well had been installed in 1900. 'Bubbles' Pratley and her parents lived in the further cottage for a time, and she remembers what life was like then. *'Every household was fairly self-sufficient with hens in the back garden and vegetables and fruit home grown or from the allotment. Potatoes were in clamps of earth and straw but if the winter was very severe it was impossible to open the clamps. Runner beans were salted, and eggs preserved in isinglass. (I did not much enjoy these.) Most families kept a pig. Our diet was quite stodgy, based mainly on suet puddings (butcher's suet) which were sweet or savoury.'* The drip moulds around the windows indicate a much earlier building. There were two more on the rear wall which, when these cottages were demolished in the 1960s, were combined to make a window for the reconstructed house, 8 Fox Lane, built in their place.

The Old Malt House

There had been a malt house on the site of 5 Fox Lane since the early 18th century and the last maltster in Barton, Mrs Haynes, continued malting until the 1880s. After that William Preston carried on his saddlery business here. Malting had been done in a building pulled down and replaced in 1950 by Fox Cottage.

On the verge nearby, a tree has been planted to mark the position of the stocks. which were removed in 1868. The fastening is said to be that now used on the gate into the churchyard.

Enstone Road

The Fox, at the junction of Fox Lane and Enstone Road, was a licensed public house in 1812 and in 1819 was bought by William Hall, brewer, from Thomas Chilton for £820 and £10 for the fixtures.

Mark Stockford senior was the licensee between 1895 and 1899, and his wife was standing by the door in this photograph. A long tenancy was held by the Gooding family from 1911 to 1964. Twenty five years later, the pub was closed and up for sale, but it was rescued and, with Vito Logozzi as licensee, has been refurbished and extended and now includes a restaurant.

A view looking east along the road from The Fox. This was another of the Kirby, c1920, photographs. On the left was the Castle family workshop. Three generations of the family worked here as wheelwrights, builders and undertakers. Their bill for a funeral in 1928 was £6 12s 6d.

The building on the right was a house with a shop (fish, general stores, then a butcher's) and two adjacent cottages. The cottages are now one cottage, the home of the author of this book. At the time the photograph was taken, the two cottages had their gardens and their privies on the other side of the road, now the B4030, but not quite such a busy road then!

At that time, too, the field between the cottages and The Fox was regularly used by a visiting fair. Houses and bungalows have now been built on this field and also on the site of the Castle family workshop which was demolished in 1966.

The elms can be seen in this picture, another c1920 Kirby photograph, looking west from the cross roads where the Worton and Kiddington roads come into the main road. The smaller girl is carrying a milk can. The building in the centre was the workshop of the Baker family, wheelwrights, builders and carpenters, and just beyond was the hut where 'Zach' Barrett cut hair and mended kettles. Men and boys used to gather there – in a very smoky atmosphere. These have been replaced partly by a building housing a hairdresser's and partly by the road into the Woodway estate, built in the 1960s.

The entrance to Elm Grove Farm was near the elm trees. These elms and many others in The Bartons have all gone, mainly as a result of disease and this has changed the appearance greatly. The wall on the left was removed when a layby was created with a platform on which Nat Jarvis, farming at Elm Grove then, could put his milk churns to await collection.

By 1984 the barns, their farming era over, were used for the various activities advertised on this sign. Jim Keeling had his pottery here until he moved, in that year, to Whichford near Shipston-on-Stour.

The house is now a family home and the barns have been converted into two houses and two bungalows.

Worton Road

c1915. Margaret and Josiah Wilkins outside their cottage a short way up Worton Road on the left-hand side. Four cottages here were pulled down, and the sheds put in their place were for a time used by market trader 'Dabster', whose stink bombs caused disapproval in some quarters when let off in schools. The sheds were later used by car repairers, and now a house has been built on the site.

This c1920 Kirby series view up the Worton Road, No. 6 on the right, shows a quiet country lane. A great deal of traffic now goes up and down this road, going to businesses, to the playing fields and to the houses built in the 1950s and 1960s.

There was not quite so much traffic in 1970 when this picture of Robert and John Webb was taken with their brother Ron, then at Webb's shop in Sandford, in the van which he so painstakingly converted.

Airey houses, now refurbished and given a new lease of life, were built in Hillside Road in 1953. This was followed by the building of a new estate nearby, and many village families moved here from Jacob's Yard and Fox Lane.

Hopcroft's Holt

The staff at Hopcroft's Holt garage c1936. Standing, left to right: George Kirby junior, Archie Price, Fred Price, Jack Smith (from Steeple Aston). Seated Harold Crowther, — . Fred Price set up the garage, then known as Price's Garage, soon after the First World War. Archie Price later set up his own car repair service near the entrance to Whistlow Farm between Hopcroft's Holt and the Duns Tew Road, making use of a site that in the mid-19th century had been a brick works. His house and some others nearby have now been demolished.

Hopcroft's Holt garage is just within the boundary of The Bartons. This view into the adjoining parish was taken in 1894.

Westcote Barton and the Church

The Church of St Edward the Confessor in Westcote Barton, now the only church in Oxfordshire to bear this name, is known to be on the site of a much earlier church as Saxon stone foundations were discovered in 1977.

Drawing by J C Buckler, 1823. (MS Top Oxon a 69 no 580, by permission of The Bodleian Library, Oxford)

The church looked like this and had a gallery inside when Revd Edmund Lockyer became Rector in 1852 and wrote a note in the parish banns register about a wedding in that year: *'rough noisy young men crowded into the gallery . . . making a disgraceful uproar. I was obliged to turn everyone out of the Church — except the Wedding party.'* He was not entirely sympathetic to the labouring people of the parish but he cared greatly for the church and its restoration, and it was he who repainted the rood screen.

The church was restored in 1855 by G E Street and he left much of the earlier work unchanged. The building has some 12th century stonework, but most of it is 14th and 15th century. The designs on the fine 15th century rood screen are copied in the kneelers embroidered by local people to commemorate important events in their lives.

In the churchyard is the base of a medieval cross, and looking to the south can be seen the humps and bumps and earthworks of earlier settlement. In medieval times, the buildings did not extend beyond the site of what is now Park Farm, then the manor house next to the church.

SOVTH WEST VIEW OF WESTCOTT BARTON CHVRCH.

The church after it had been altered, a drawing in *Memorials of Westcott Barton* by Jenner Marshall, published in 1870.

The gate leading from the road into the churchyard has an ironwork fastening believed to have been part of the stocks which were set up near the Fox Inn.

Drawings, by Mandy Hughes, from *The Bartons Village Appraisal*, 1993.

Inside the church is a 12th century tomb recess which has carved cable and chevron decoration.

The interior in 1968. (*The Oxford Times*)

The war memorial was put in the Church in 1930. In the following year a modern Rood, or Crucifix, was put in place of the Rood which would have been taken down at the time of the Reformation. Electric light was installed in 1934 at a cost of £36 15s 11d.

There is a blocked-up doorway on the north wall that led to the rood loft above the screen which was used for keeping the candles alight in front of the Rood. The Staffordshire floor tiles of the 1856 restoration were replaced by wooden flooring in 1977, and this provided the opportunity for the archaeological survey which discovered the Saxon foundations.

The rectory in the 1920s. It was built in 1838 for Revd S Y Seagrave who kept a sizeable establishment and was a hunting parson. Seagrave's Covert in the north of the parish was named after him.

Moses and Jim Castle with William Brain and others sawing timber in the grounds of the Rectory. The Revd R S Edwards, wearing a boater, was the Rector from 1900 to 1911. The Castle family were local builders, and William Brain was Clerk and Sexton for 56 years.

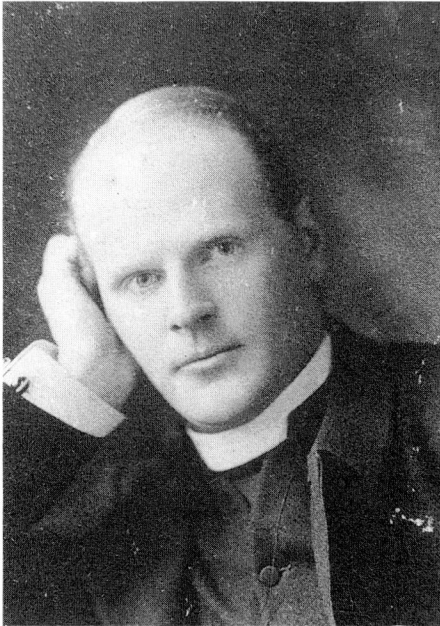

Canon Alexander William Carroll
Rector 1921–1929.

Revd Charles Henry Stuart Gmelin
Rector 1929–1938

By 1963 the rectory on the north side of the road had been sold and a smaller rectory built on the same side of the road as the church.

A carriage bridge on Enstone Hill over the river Dorn was first built when the road was made into a turnpike road in 1793. The bridge pictured here (OPA) had been rebuilt in 1868 by a local builder, William Grimsley, at a cost of £95 and, in spite of heavy lorries thundering over it, no major repairs have yet been needed.

The 'keaching' steps, used by people when they fetched water from the brook, can be seen clearly. It is believed that the group on the bridge were members of the James family, who lived in Fox Lane, and that the picture was taken in 1924.

The thatched part of the first cottage beyond the bridge, Burnside, still looks much the same, although the lower part has now been made into a two-storey building. The three-storeyed Hennock House, hidden by creeper, may at one time, back in the 1790s, have been a pub called The White Horse.

Just beyond the houses in the photograph was the house, at the end of a drive (Cocksparrow Hall), where Dorothy Sayers's son came soon after this photograph was taken, to live with other children. Ivy Shrimpton, who looked after them there, called her house 'The Sidelings' after the name of the field on which it was built in 1727, but that name is now used for the house by the roadside. The names Sparrow or Cocksparrow Hill were sometimes used for this stretch of road.

Footpaths across the fields would have been used by people living here and in the cotteges further up the hill when they walked to the shops in the centre of the village.

A view, 1950s, looking the other way, back towards the turning to Sandford St Martin from the main road. The house in the centre is Brookside and the buildings of Park Farm are on the right.

The back view of Manor Farm cottages in the Sandford road in the 1920s.

In the 18th century the Buswell family had come to live in Westcote Barton. These were prosperous times and members of the family rebuilt many houses and built houses further to the west. These cottages belonged to them, and they also built their new manor house in the Sandford Road, the house that is now Manor Farm.

By the mid-19th century there were no Buswells here, and houses and land had been bought by the Revd Jenner Marshall who had a manor house built even further west. He was a clergyman but did not hold a cure. The farms he owned were let to tenant farmers. Manor Farm was let to Arthur Bosley and Park Farm, next to the church, was let to Fred Taylor. When the Marshall estate was sold in the mid-20th century, both farms were bought by those tenants, and members of the families have continued to farm the land.

Manor Farm had a prize-winning herd of British Friesians until recently and the cows had to be milked every morning and every evening. The milking has come to an end; there are no cows now, and both farms are mainly arable with an added interest, particularly at Park Farm, in horses.

Revd Jenner and Elizabeth Kelson Marshall pictured, c1900, outside their house, Westcote Barton Manor.

During the Second World War, the Manor House was used as a Land Army Hostel. The Rector, the Revd William Lindsay, commented in the Woodstock Ruridecanal Magazine, January 1949: *'These young persons were a help to the social life of the district and will be missed, although unfortunately their thoughts and footsteps did not appear to turn much in the direction of the Church.'*

In 1964, George and Cynthia Laws were living in the Manor House and they held a reunion when ex-Land Army girls, several now married to local men, met the farmers for whom they had worked. Left to right, back: George and Cynthia Laws. Farmers: Fred Taylor, Henry Hunt, Raymond Goffe, J H Hughes, J L Kearsey, Arthur Bosley, Thomas Henman. (*The Oxford Times*)

George Laws, who died in 1972, did a lot of work on village history and his research has formed the basis of later work.

Steeple Barton and the Church

'The view from this room is small, but it . . . contains in its detail something of every age from the Saxon to the nineteenth century.' (W G Hoskins, *The Making of the English Landscape,* 1955, by permission of Hodder & Stoughton.) Professor Hoskins wrote this while he was living in the Old Vicarage in Steeple Barton.

There are only a few houses now in Steeple Barton, but there are many traces of earlier dwellings. There was certainly a church here in the 12th century and probably much earlier. The present building dates from the 14th century when there was a thriving agricultural community near the church but, soon afterwards, this came to an end and people moved a mile away to Middle Barton. The church is now in a quiet and peaceful setting surrounded by fields, but it is still the parish church for most of the people living in Middle Barton.

Drawing by J C Buckler, 1823. (MS Top Oxon a 68 no 513, by permission of The Bodleian Library, Oxford)

The 14th century pillars inside the church have carved heads, and one has the unusual feature of linked arms.

Drawings, by Peter Winchester, from *The Bartons Village Appraisal,* 1993.

A drawing of the church after it had been altered in 1855 to the designs of J C Buckler. These pictures of the church and of the vicarage were drawn in about 1870, but it is not known who the artist was. The pictures belonged to the Baker family and it is possible that they were given to Solomon Baker, instead of payment, when he was the licensee of The Three Horseshoes, one of the village pubs. (The pictures are now in the Oxfordshire County Council Photographic Archive.)

The interior, decorated at harvest time in 1988, photographed by John Madden.

Henry Luing was clerk and sexton for fifty years until 1887. One of his sons, Alfred, emigrated to America when he married in 1862 and founded a Luing dynasty there. Letters from father to son give information about Steeple Barton and, in particular, about the installation of the fine organ in Steeple Barton church. Members of the family in America visit this country and keep in touch with descendants here.

Henry Luing's son William followed in his footsteps as clerk and held the position for thirty years.

The Vicarage, shown in this drawing of c1870, was built in 1856 and designed by S S Teulon. The land agent William Wing, in 1866 in his *Annals of Steeple Barton and Westcot Barton,* commented: *'The architect being a Londoner, overlooked the necessity of providing a country clergyman with a stable and piggery. Notwithstanding this oversight the design and execution of Steeple Barton vicarage possesses considerable merit.'* Now known as The Old Vicarage, it replaced an earlier building that had fallen into disrepair. The monkey puzzle tree had to be cut down in the 1940s.

Many of the vicars held the living in conjunction with livings elsewhere, and one, Robert Wright, Vicar from 1808 to 1850, is said to have visited the parish only once.

In 1904, an unusual appointment was made. Revd Simon Stephen was believed to be an Armenian and named Shimoun Stephan Isko when he was born in Mosul, then in the Turkish Empire. He studied at the Sorbonne and was a Doctor of Divinity. He was a Roman Catholic priest before becoming a Protestant and came to Steeple Barton in 1904 where he was Vicar until he died in 1946. He was well regarded and long remembered by his parishioners as approachable if eccentric. During his time there was a Sunday school, and a choir that took part in many musical performances.

The benefices of Steeple Barton and Westcote Barton were united in 1960 and became a United Benefice with Sandford St Martin and Duns Tew in 1977. The incumbent has oversight of all four parishes but, though Rector of Westcote Barton, he is still Vicar of Steeple Barton.

Men and boys outnumbered women in the choir in 1924. Left to right, back row: Bert Thomas, — Wheeler, Charles Marsh, Walter Parsons, Ronnie Riach, Bert Farley, George Stockford, Solomon Stewart, Pop Hopes, Robert Harper?, William John Constable, Percival Grimsley. Middle row: —, Bessie Stockford, —, Geraldine Gibson, Kate Gertrude Parsons. Front row: Aubrey West, Ellis Farley, Bill Irons, Bob Jarvis. Boys: believed to include Walter Boffin, John Boffin, — Knight, Albert Bolton, Ben Stockford, Don Stockford.

Choirboys on Steeple Barton church tower, late 1940s. Left to right: Ronnie Gibson, John Fowler, Robin Cox, Michael Hazell, David Jarvis, Brian (Danny) Stockford, Arthur Cattle.

The Green Bartonicas, a harmonica band, was started in the 1930s just before the war at St Mary's Sunday School and was in existence until the early 1940s. Members wore white shirts with green ties and green berets. The band gave concerts here and also travelled outside the village to play at hospitals and the workhouse, which still existed then. The signature tune was 'The Wearing of the Green'.

Left to right, standing: Ruby Pratley, Peter Hazell, Jack Eaglestone, Norman Cross, Derek Pritchard, Violet Butcher, Joyce Pritchard, Derrick Jarvis, Lydia Cross. Seated: Bill Hawkins, Charlie Hazell, Roy Pratley, Aubrey (Rock) West, Gillian Butcher, Ann Fleming, Peggy Hawker.

A drawing of Barton Abbey, c1870, probably by the same artist who drew the church and the vicarage.

A 1920s photograph (OPA) shows the house after the rebuilding of the 1890s. Above the pillars was an inscription UNLESS THE LORD BUILD THE HOUSE THEY LABOUR IN VAIN THAT BUILD IT. The inscription was removed some time during the 1920s.

The house, never an abbey, was built in Elizabethan times for the Dormer family who soon after that moved to Rousham. In 1822 it was sold to William Hall of the Swan Brewery, Oxford, and over the next hundred years the Hall family built up an estate and enlarged the house. It was they who gave it the name of Barton Abbey.

Joseph and Frances Pike lived here for ten years and then Philip Fleming, a banker, came with his wife Joan in 1933. Their son Robin and his wife Vicky live in Steeple Barton, and alterations have recently been made to Barton Abbey for the benefit of their elder son. The Hall and Fleming families have both been generous benefactors to the church and to the village.

Alexander William Hall, 1838–1919, (*The Oxford Times Centenary Supplement,* 1962) He held many public appointments; he was MP for Oxford 1874–1880 and 1885–1892, though Oxford was disfranchised during the years between because of his electioneering malpractice. He was a member of the Oxfordshire County Council, and became chairman of various committees, including the education committee. He was also involved with rural district council matters and, locally, with the parish council, with local charities, church affairs and with the school he provided for the village.

Joan Fleming, who died in 1991 aged 89, was a well-known horsewoman who won numerous trophies with horses she bred, rode and trained. Visitors to the stables at Barton Abbey used to admire the great number of rosettes covering several walls in the stable block. She was active during the Second World War in the Red Cross and also ran a tea car that took refreshments to troops and people in blitzed areas. For many years she organised horse shows, with much of the money raised being given to local causes.

Chapel

A chapel in The Bartons was first recorded in 1814. By the mid-19th century there were two, one was Primitive Methodist and the other Wesleyan Methodist. The religious census of 1851 listed three but such is the confusion about the names of the different parts of The Bartons that the Wesleyan chapel appears to have been entered twice, one entry by the Superintendent at Chipping Norton and the other by the local steward, with slightly different figures being given!

The Wesleyan chapel was in Worton Road, but it is not known where the 1851 Primitive Methodist chapel was, although oral tradition suggests that it may have been a building in Westcote Barton in the drive to Manor Farm. Shortly after the census was taken, a chapel was built in Fox Lane and nine years later, in 1860, was made into a house (10 Fox Lane). It was then that the Primitive Methodists built the chapel in The Dock which, still in use today, is one of the few remaining Methodist churches in North Oxfordshire.

The chapel as it was in 1930. (OPA) The poplar trees were still there but we know from the Woodstock Ruridecanal Magazine that 'trees fell in abundance during a gale' in February 1930, and they are believed to have fallen then. Just visible in the photograph is the wall of the cottages adjoining the chapel. Two cottages and a plot of land were purchased by the chapel trustees in 1860 and the chapel was built against the wall of one of the cottages. Details of the purchase exist but no information has been found about the actual building of the chapel. The cottages are no longer there. They were finally pulled down in 1953, but marks on the chapel wall show where the adjoining cottage had been.

The interior was modernised in 1984, and this photograph shows what it had been like before this.

On the wall, above the pulpit, was the text O GIVE THANKS UNTO THE LORD FOR HE IS GOOD. A small entrance lobby had doors on either side leading into the chapel. Between the doors facing into the chapel, was a cupboard. An interior wall has now been built and there is an entrance lobby with a separate room and a kitchen. Pews have been replaced by chairs and there is a carpet on the floor. Tablets on the wall remain. These are dedicated to Hilare, who was a daughter of Henry and Catherine Hall at the local 'big house' Barton Abbey, and her husband John de Burgh Rochfort. The Rochforts were particularly active in chapel life and he was a preacher, but other members of the Hall family gave support to chapel as well as to church.

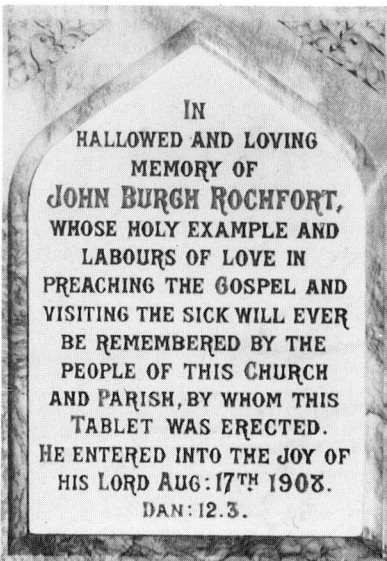

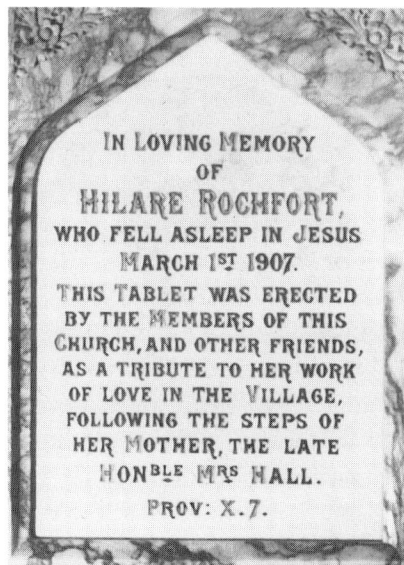

The Wesleyan Methodist chapel was in Worton Road, then more usually known as Chapel Street. In 1932, the Primitive Methodists and Wesleyan Methodists joined together and formed the Methodist Church.

The Wesleyan chapel in Worton Road, c1930. Ten years later the chapel closed and during the war the building was used for storage. After the war, it was converted into a house, 2 Worton Road.

Messrs. J. Stewart G. Kirby	BARTON (South St.)...	2 30
	"	6 0
	Wednesday	7 0
Mr. W. Howe	BARTON (Worton Rd.)	6 0
	Tuesday	7 0

Information about both chapels, with the number of members on the right, was given in The Chipping Norton and Stow Methodist Circuit Plan of 1940.

Ruth Kirby recalled activities in the 1920s and 1930s. *'Many of my memories are of the Methodist Chapel which in those days was Primitive Methodist. Years spent in Sunday School when old Mr. Matthews was Superintendent, and later my father and later still Mr Castle whom I used to help. Also years spent playing the organ. Sunday was a busy day then. Prayer Meeting at 7. Sunday School 10.30. Dash off to play at the Wesleyan Chapel at 11. Sunday School 1.30 followed by Service 2.30 and again at 6. We did lots of singing in those days. And in the week there was Fellowship Monday night, Christian Endeavour Wednesday, Women's Meeting Thursday, Prayer Meeting Friday night. Lots of special events, Tea Meetings, Sunday School Outings. All this seemed to change when the war came.'*

The Sunday School outings were major events, for both children and grown ups. For many it was their only opportunity of a day at the seaside. Up to the 1920s people set off at about 5 a.m. and walked over two miles to Heyford Station to catch the train, had a day by the sea and then walked back from Heyford when they returned in the early hours of the following day. The school and shops closed on the day of the outing, and attendance at school was low on the following day. By the 1940s, travel was by coach.

An outing to Wicksteed Park in the 1930s. Left to right, back row: Betty Bolton, –, Ella Reeves, Dorothy Wood, –, Pat Probbitts, Barbara Bolton, Alec Stewart. Middle row: John Stevens, Nigel Wood, Eric Portlock, June Shirley, Cyril Shirley, Horace Wood, Rita Stewart, Kathie Bolton (in hat). Front row: Poppy Broom, Jean Carpenter, Heather Portlock, Dora Gibson, Roy Eaglestone, Sylvia Portlock, Violet Taylor.

Graham and Cynthia Bradshaw with Ruth Kirby on an outing to the seaside in the 1950s. Graham Bradshaw later made drawings of the village and many paintings of birds and animals.

Charles Hawtin and Lily Castle, both Primitive Methodists, were married in 1910. Left to right, back row: Jesse, Jane, Mabel, William Stewart, Elsie Claridge?, Aggie Adams, Hilary Stewart, –, Mary Matthews (Mrs Teddy). Middle row: Deborah Stewart (Mrs Will), Winnie and Elsie Reeves?, –, Tom Castle, Ken Castle, James Castle, Emma (Cherry), Moses Castle, Horace Castle, Solomon Stewart (from Canada), Archie Reeves, Teddy Matthews, Alfred Reeves. Front row: Will Stewart, George H Kirby, –, – Hawtin, Charles and Lily Hawtin, Annie Castle, – Stewart. Kneeling: Fred Reeves, Bert Stewart. The chapel band played at the wedding, and was photographed at the same time.

The Chapel or Mission Band in 1910.

Left to right, back row: Fred Reeves, Will Stewart, Solomon Stewart (from Canada), Jim Castle, Alfred Reeves (with drum), Ken Castle, Charlie Hawtin, Bert Stewart, Horace Castle, Teddy Matthews. Seated: Archie Reeves, George Kirby.

Open air Camp Meetings were held in the summer, and the band led people round the village. They usually started at The Green in South Street, but sometimes began at Chapel House in Fox Lane, because there had once been a chapel there. People also went to meetings in other villages. Mont Abbott's comment about such a meeting is recorded by Sheila Stewart in *Lifting the Latch,* 1987 (by permission of Oxford University Press). *'Mr Kirby from Barton were a topping preacher perched up high on an old wagon with Barton Band.'*

School

The school is in Church Lane, on the edge of the built up area, and this Kirby photograph shows it as it was in 1920 with the 'mound' and trees at the side. The land and buildings were provided by Alexander William Hall of Barton Abbey, and the date, 1866, is shown in a datestone on the south-facing wall. It was a National, or Church school, and was known as Steeple Barton Church of England Schools, the schools being the Infants School and the Mixed School for older boys and girls. Children from both Steeple Barton and Westcote Barton parishes went to the school. In 1921 the school was handed over to the Oxfordshire Education Authority and it then ceased to be a church school. The name was not changed until 1953 when it became Middle Barton County Primary School.

A hall, for assemblies and gymnastics, was added in 1959 and new classrooms in 1968 and 1971. It is an interesting building, ironstone and limestone used in bands, with a bell cote and attractive finials on roof pinnacles. The building has been well maintained by the Local Education Authority and well looked after by staff and pupils. When the school opened, there were 90 pupils, and by 1891 the numbers had gone up to 216. Numbers had decreased by the 1930s, but have gone up again as a result of new housing being built, and now remain steady at about 150.

The log-books, records kept by headteachers, are a splendid source of information about school events and also about village life. There were entries each year, similar to this one, about the harvest holiday: 1906 Aug 3 *'Closed school for Harvest holidays. Five weeks.'* School holidays were at the same time as the harvest — sometimes earlier in the summer, sometimes later. This gives us an indication of the importance of children's help for bringing in the harvest.

c1905. Children on their way to or from school. Left to right: Miriam Gibson, Joe Stockford, Dolly Beale, −, Gertrude Simson. The river Dorn, or the brook as it is usually called, runs though the village. There is a ford here in Mill Lane, and one in Fox Lane. Both have footbridges, and in between is a road bridge and another footbridge. There used to be more water in the brook and, in heavy rain, the level rose quickly. Children were often unable to cross from the north side of the brook to the school which is on the south side. There were many entries in the school log-books like this one. 1908 Apr 28 *Owing to heavy rain the brook rose in flood. We were obliged to cancel the attendance and send the children home.*

1937. A group by the mound. The mound has gone and the school hall is here now. Right to left, back row: −, Ian Thomas, Jean Carpenter, Betty Bolton, Roy Pratley, Roy Eaglestone, Gertie Gibson. Middle row: Eileen Probbitts, −, Cyril Shirley, Cathy Bolton, −, −, Di Jarvis. Front row: Tony Moulder, Jack Hazell. Ian Thomas went on to design clothes and, for 23 years, was the Queen's dressmaker.

Numbers at the school were augmented during war-time by evacuees. By 1940, there were 98 children on the school roll; 48 were Oxfordshire children and 50 were evacuees. School children helped the war effort by picking nettles, rose hips and blackberries, by collecting bones and giving concerts to raise money.

A war-time class with evacuees as well as local children 1939. Miss Faint, who was not at the school for long, was the teacher, Kenneth Colvert was one of the evacuees and local children included: Left to right, back row: Jack Hazell. Middle row: Stella Gibson, Arthur Gamage, Cyril Shirley, June Halsey, Marion Hazell. Front row: −, Hilary Blackwell, Doreen Gascoigne, Eileen Probbitts, Poppy Broom, Di Jarvis, −, −. Tony Moulder was just behind Miss Faint on her left.

Martin Norton, headteacher, with a recorder group at a concert in the school hall in 1988 when a presentation was made to Joan Sullivan on her retirement as chairman of the school governors. The players included left to right: Kelly Webb, Nicola Portlock, Carl Peedell, Kathryn Hanks, Andrew McAdam, James Baskerville, Dawn Arnold teacher, (violin).

A football team in 1984 wearing shorts and jerseys bought with the money raised in a sponsored fish organised by Vic Squire. Left to right, back row: Paul Tumman, Michael Beale, Ben Squire, Mark Parrett, Dean Fowler, Christopher Payne, Richard Hudson. Front row: Richard Golder, Simon Mills, Sam Monk, Carl Field, Michael Goss, Luke Morgan.

Pupils pictured in 1986 with their new minibus. Money to buy it was raised by pupils and the Parent Teacher Association with the help of members of the local community, and the PTA takes responsibility for maintenance and running costs. Part of the single-storey classroom block can be seen at the back of the picture with the Playgroup, now Pre-school, building beyond.

In 1988, the opening of the new garage for the minibus was celebrated by maypole dancing. In the foreground were Lauren Morgan and Marc Newman. (*Banbury Guardian*)

Pre-school

Playgroup, as it used to be called, started in a private house in 1967 and moved to Sandford St Martin village hall two years later with the children being transported by minibus. In 1974 it returned to Barton and met in the Alice Marshall Hall. Then, ten years later, after much energetic fundraising, a new building next to the school was opened. This achievement was recognised by a Village Ventures award.

Helpers and children at the new building in 1985 soon after winning the award. (*The Oxford Times*) Left to right, adults: Sarah Pinion, Dorothy Allen, Muriel Standen, Sonia Norgrove, Eryl Connolly, Sue Wetherall. Children: Eleanor Norgrove, Vanessa and Carl Standen, Lucy Waring, David Connolly. Back view: Victoria Pinion, –, –.

A Mother, Baby or Toddlers group was set up in 1974 and this, now called Busy Bees, meets regularly in the Alice Marshall Hall.

Alice Marshall Hall

The village hall was built as a Church Mission and Temperance Hall and it is this name, with the date 1888, which is inscribed on the wall. The hall was established to counter the attractions of the public houses, and fundraising was carried out principally by Miss Alice Marshall, daughter of Revd Jenner Marshall, of Westcote Barton Manor House.

Church Mission and Temperance Hall,
MIDDLE BARTON.
(in a very poor open Village in Oxfordshire.)

£ *48* — *still required on the Building, and funds are also much needed for the furnishing.*

ALL HELP MOST THANKFULLY RECEIVED.

Christmas Offerings earnestly solicited.

The following Attractive Articles, sold in aid of the above, are suitable for CHRISTMAS PRESENTS & BIRTHDAY GIFTS, and sell readily at Bazaars, etc.—

SILVER BROOCHES AND SCARF PINS,
AND
LARGE HOLLAND APRONS.

For Price please see other side.

Kindly pass on this Paper, and recommend.

4125 Aprons have been sold.
3675 Brooches and Scarf Pins have been sold.

Please address to the Hon Treasurer,
Miss A. S. MARSHALL,
Westcott Barton,
Near Oxford.

☞ **Orders most earnestly solicited.**
Please, DO send.

The money was raised and the hall was built. The site chosen was at the cross roads in the centre of the village where the two parishes adjoin each other. At that time, traffic was no problem. Now, with limited parking space and the widespread use of cars, there are difficulties.

The hall c1920. (OPA) It had been built by H R Franklin of Deddington at a cost, in 1888, of £619 12s 3d, with an extra £80 for furniture, and it has been used ever since by most of the local organisations. It has been the scene of many discussions on village policies. The first Steeple Barton Parish Council meeting was held here in 1894 when about one hundred people turned up to elect their committee. Since then, the council and other bodies have met regularly to discuss village matters. Long serving chairmen of the Parish Council and Parish meeting include Alexander William Hall, Charles Marsh, Walter Howe, Norman Cross, Eric Pratley, Joan Irons, Jenner and Francis Eden Marshall, and those serving on the local district council have included Swynfen Jarvis, Kenneth Bauckham, Isabel and Joan Sullivan, John Fergie, Charles Cunningham, Geoffrey Bosley, Arthur Goffe.

Entertainments and social gatherings also take place in the hall. Joan Fleming and Mary Osment were among members of the Red Cross who organised this tea party in the hall in the 1940s. Those sitting at the table included Rose West, Rene Stockford, James Canty, Pop Hopes.

Information about the hall was given in a note published when a new doorway, the one in use today, was opened in Coronation Year, 1937. At that time, too, when the doorway was proposed, this sketch map of the hall was drawn by Swynfen Jervis.

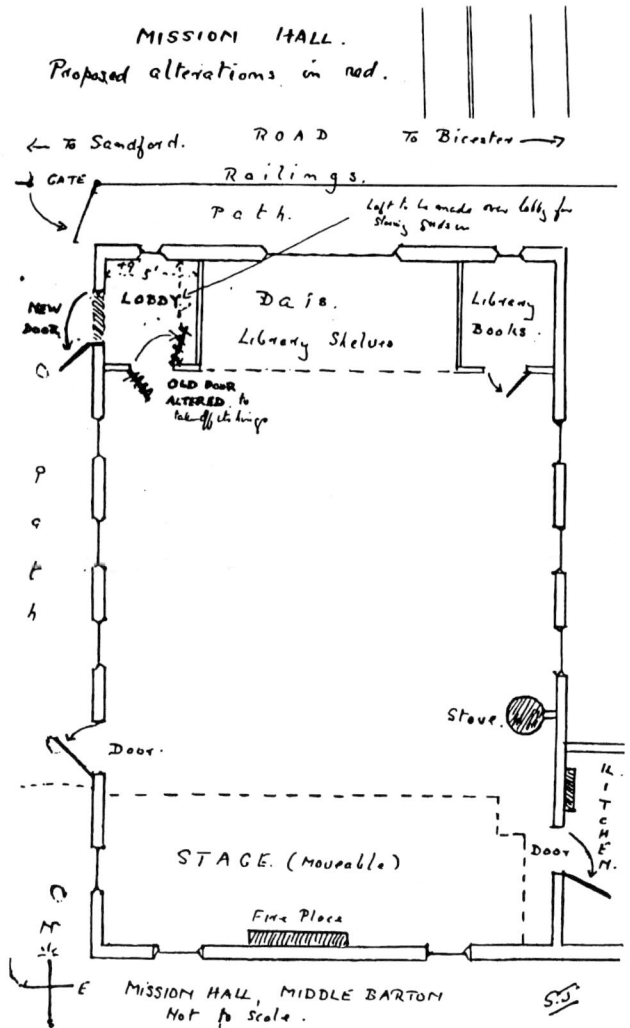

MISSION   HALL.

Proposed alterations in red.

← To Sandford.   ROAD   To Bicester →

GATE   Railings.

Path.

LOBBY   Daïs.   Library
NEW   Books.
DOOR   Library Shelves

OLD DOOR
ALTERED to
take off its hinge

Stove.

Door.

STAGE. (Moveable.)

Door

Fire Place

MISSION HALL, MIDDLE BARTON
Not to scale.

Activities in the hall were recalled by 'Bubbles' Pratley when the centenary of the hall was celebrated. *'In the mid-1920s, the hall was the focal point of the social life of the villagers of Middle Barton, with paraffin lamps, no water supply, coke stove with white stone hearth, one outside very small vault lavatory.*

The serving hatch end of the hall was lined with bookshelves, this being the lending library. The pig club held meetings, also the Women's Institute. There were many concerts, children's and adult, choral singing practice, whist drives (as many as 20 tables) film shows, parties and receptions. Wedding receptions took place without an alcoholic toast as the 'temperance' was strictly adhered to and it was usual for the guests to gather afterwards at the house of the bride for 'the toast'.

War came and the Army took over the hall as a cookhouse and the barrels of beer rolled through the hall door! After the troops moved on, the 'temperance' ban was gradually ignored.'

It was not, however, until 1966 that the ban was finally lifted. A new committee, representing village organisations, was set up and it was then that the hall, in memory of the fundraising, was re-named the Alice Marshall Hall.

Bartons Victory Memorial Hall and Playing Fields

This building & playing fields
were made possible by
the people of the Bartons.
In appreciation of those who served
& in memory of those who gave their lives
in the 1939–1945 war

Plaque at the Sports and Social Club.

The playing fields, in the centre of the village alongside Worton Road, were created in 1948. Money to buy the land was raised during the war, and generous help was given by Major Philip Fleming of Barton Abbey. The Memorial Hall Fund, a registered charity for the benefit of all people in The Bartons, owns the land and buildings, and the Sports and Social Club uses them to promote sporting and social activities.

A hall was not built then; but a wooden sports pavilion, brought here from the Wootton Hundred Tennis Club at Hopcroft's Holt, was put up.

1950s team in front of the pavilion. Left to right, back row: Robin Cox, Ron Gascoigne, John Bolton, John Fowler, Derrick Jarvis, David Jarvis. Seated: Bill Dempsey, Brian Coker, Tony Smith, Glyn Cox, Peter Bauckham.

By the 1970s, the pavilion was in need of repair and there were discussions about replacing it or even building a community centre in the playing fields. That scheme came to nothing, and members of the Football Club set to and themselves built the club room which is the focal point of the Sports and Social Club. The Jubilee room was added in 1977, and a large car park provided.

Bowls played an important part in the sporting life of the village and, in 1953, a new green was opened in the playing fields. Major Philip Fleming bowled the first wood in 1953. Left to right, back row: Bill Stewart, Bob Jarvis, Revd James Wilmot Griffiths, Walter Moulder, Frank Gascoigne, Sid Cox, Tom Cattle, Arthur Perkins, 'Mac' Adams. Front row: Val Gardner, the man on the right was a county representative.

Frank Gascoigne, who worked as a blacksmith until he was in his 90s, also tended the green for many years. Since then, other enthusiasts have maintained it, and the green has been given 'starred' rating. This makes it of a high enough standard for county matches, and the Bowls Club now has its own club building.

A cricket pitch at the playing fields was in use for about ten years, but after that people from Barton joined with the players at Sandford St Martin Cricket Club. The playing fields also provide tennis courts which are used by senior and junior players. There are, too, Sunday morning meetings of the Radio Controlled Vehicles Racing Club which attract members from outside the area.

Indoor activities in the Club include pool, table tennis, dances, discos. The British Legion and the Youth Club meet there, also the Jubilee Club, which caters for seniors. There are many social gatherings and the Club facilities and playing fields are often used for village events.

Sports and Activities

Bowls

Bowls players were winning matches during the 1920s and 1930s. The green then was in the grounds of the Rectory, and a path led to it from the road opposite The Fox. Two 1930s photographs give an indication of the number of players involved and the number of cups won. No women players then.

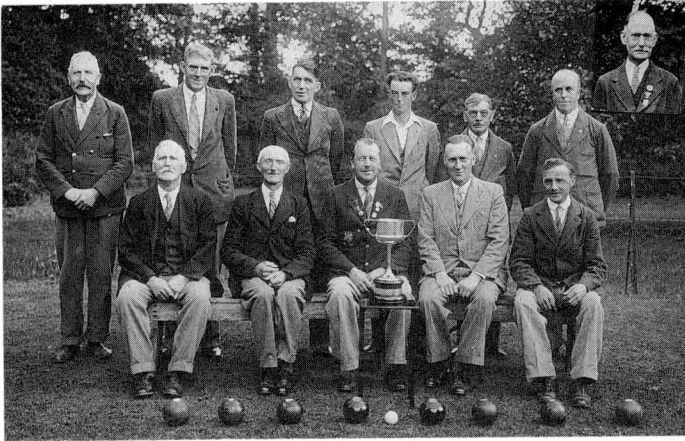

Left to right, back row: Walter Parsons, Will West, Walter Moulder, Charlie Gibbons, Jethro Callow, Bill Courtnell. Front row: James Canty, George Brooks, Ronnie Riach, Gilbert Newman, Charles Boffin. Inset: Albert Paine.

Left to right, back row: Walter Parsons, Walter Howe, Albert Paine, George Hope, Ronnie Riach, Jethro Callow. Front row: James Canty, George Brooks, Frank Gascoigne, Bill Courtnell. Seated: Alec Stewart, Gilbert Newman.

The Bowls Club, today, has men and women members. Matches are played to a high standard and competitions are held which attract players from all over Oxfordshire.

Football

Footballers, who had previously made use of a field at Sycamore Farm, moved to the playing fields and won many trophies. There was great support for the teams; the matches were a highlight of the week and a talking point for the rest of the time.

1960s, Left to right, back row: Ted Harper, Charlie Gibbons, Bob Shroder, Kenneth Bauckham, William Wood, Herman Brain. Third row: Johnnie Brookes, Bob Stewart, Robin Cox, Tom Bolton, Ron Gascoigne, Ralph Millin, Derrick Jarvis, Mervyn Cox, David Jarvis, George Hughes. Second row: Ian Lowden, Glyn Cox, Brian Coker, Tony Smith, John Fowler, Bill Dempsey, Peter Bauckham, Jim Moulder. Front row: Derek Gardner, 'Titch' Simmonds.

1965–1966. Bob Rose six-a-side winners. Left to right, back row: Ron Gascoigne, Len Panting, Derrick Jarvis. Front row: Michael Thomas, Bob Shirley, Peter Wetherall.

Football continues to be popular and successful today. The teams are doing well and league trophies are being won.

Boys football team, 1970, winners of the Wootton Junior League Cup. Left to right, back row: Brian (Danny) Stockford, Charlie Pearce, Norman Monk, Dennis Allen. Boys: Trevor Stewart, Shaun Axtenn, John Bunce, Edmund Sokol, Tim Fowler, John Gamage, David Monk, Stephen Monk, Colin Brown, Richard Wood, Andrew Longshore.

Cricket

The Bletchington v Barton cricket match in 1924 at The Sands, Steeple Barton. The building, recently restored and re-thatched, is in the field to the east of Barton Abbey. The man in the trilby hat was Sidney Cox and, next to him also in white, was Owen Benfield. Seated: Jethro Callow, Tom Hazell. J Newman?, Jack Thomas.

A 1950s team at the newly opened playing fields. Left to right, back row: Peter Bauckham, Jack Cox, Arthur Stevens, George Hughes, Robin Cox, Derrick Jarvis, Ron Gascoigne. Front row: Bill Gascoigne, Derek Gardner, Ralph Millin, Jim Moulder, Sid Brock.

The cricket pitch did not, however, remain for long at the playing fields and Barton cricketers now play at Sandford St Martin Cricket Club. The teams are successful in Banbury and League matches.

1988. Left to right, back row: Steve Cox, Steve Cook, Steve Harris, James Michelmore, Nigel Gillingham, Mark Robey. Front row: Martin Anson, Dave Panting, Paul Tew (captain), Rob Taylor, Chas Taylor. Brothers Rob and Chas Taylor, from Park Farm, were two of the six Barton members of the team and Chas was soon afterwards playing in county cricket.

Women's Institute

WI members also, at one time, played cricket. It is reported that two of the players took out their false teeth before venturing on to the pitch.

Pictured in the 1950s at The Sands at Steeple Barton. Left to right, back row: Barbara Wood, Hilda Cox, Ada Stockford, Marjorie Irons, 'Bubbles' Pratley, Hilda Gascoigne, Mary Osment. Front row: Mary West, Brenda Monk, a stable girl, Cicely Castle, Jill Butler.

The Bartons branch of the WI was formed in 1923 and has held regular meetings since then. It has played an active part in village affairs, particularly in war time when members organised the placing and welfare of evacuees, ran national savings groups, preserved 2745 pounds of fruit, collected herbs and set to work on an allotment to grow vegetables. The Christmas parties, one for adults and one for children, were very popular events. Members could each take one visitor and the following comment was made. *'The parties are a highlight of village life, and we all try to make friends with a WI member.'*

Members who took part in a handicraft exhibition in 1966. Left to right: Sybil Turner, Mary West, Florence Simons, Mary Osment, Ruby Pratley, Nellie Probbitts, Gwendolyn Wilmot Griffiths, Nellie Cattle. (*The Oxford Times*)

A meeting in 1966. (*The Oxford Times*) Left to right, back row: Nita Watts, Ruth Hosier. Third row: −, Astra Donaghy, −, − Isaacson, Mary West. Second row: Joan Sullivan, Florence Simons, Mary West (Sandford), Evelyn Rye, Kathleen Packard. Front row: Sybil Turner, Hilda Cox, −, Harriet Evans. Front row: Sue Lock, Gill Woolley, Win Jarvis.

The WI Golden Jubilee was celebrated in 1973 − this gathering was at the school − and two founder members, Delia Stockford (née Carroll) and Mona Owen (née Kirby) came back to the village for the celebration. Since then, the Diamond Jubilee and the 75th anniversary have been celebrated − in 1983 and 1998.

Scouts and Guides

Harry Bassett was in this group of Barton Scouts at the Wembley Jamboree in 1924 with their Scoutmaster Colonel Swynfen Jervis who was also District Commissioner. He ran Cubs as well, helped by Delia Carroll, daughter of the Rector, and then he worked with Joan Sullivan in the 1930s when she became Cub Master.

Cubs in 1933. Left to right: Bunty Simson, —, —, Ernest Gamage, Charlie Hazell.

Serving the refreshments at a Scout Jamboree at Westcote Barton, probably in 1927.

Reports in 1930 about Scouts in the Woodstock Ruridecanal Magazine give sidelights on their activities. September: *The Troop went to St Issey near Padstow for a 12 day camp. The return journey from Wadebridge was facilitated by the kindness of the GWR who stopped their Exeter–York express at Heyford at 7.20 p.m. on purpose for the Troop to detrain.'* October: 'A trek cart has been given to the Bartons by the Cassington Troop. This is a most useful addition to their transport, being on pneumatic tyres.'

By 1946, boys were going to Steeple Aston but Scouts and Cubs started again here in 1976, have been active since then and were joined by a Venture Scout Unit in 1984.

Mona Kirby in her Guide uniform in 1925 soon after a Barton company had been formed. It was, however, only in existence for a few years. A company was formed again in 1976, four years after a Brownie pack had been started. Regular and successful meetings are now held, in uniforms that, like those of Scouts and Cubs, are different from those worn in the 1920s.

Drama, Music and Ballet

Youth clubs have met from time to time and the youth club in the 1960s, under the leadership of Jeanne and Stan Allington, made its name in the world of drama.

Middle Barton Youngsters Do it Again !

Middle Barton Youth Club have done it again !

The drama group of this lively North Oxfordshire club, judged the best from clubs in the Banbury and Chipping Norton areas, took part in the County Youth drama final at Littlemore Grammar School on Saturday week and were the winners.

THIRD TIME.

In 1963, the club won the Oxfordshire Youth Service Drama Festival competition for the third time (*Banbury Guardian*), and the cast were all congratulated on their performances. The play was 'A Pound on Demand' by Sean O'Casey, and the producer and stage manager were Eric Pratley and Vaughan Castle. The Youth Club was not allowed to compete again as they were winning too often.

The winners with their trophy. Left to right: Geoff Perkins, Eric Pratley, Julia Hope, Helena Shroder, Michael Pratley, Chris Perkins.

NEW DORNE VALLEY

MODERN COUNTRY MUSIC

LES NEWMAN STEEPLE ASTON 40250

Michael Newman, Bryan Tyrrell, Clive Watts, Bill Schanche. In front: Kenny Woodward in the 1980s.

This country band started in the 1960s as the Dorne Valley Boys, but by the 1980s, with the passing of time, had changed their name. They still draw regular audiences here, at the Sports and Social Club, and elsewhere.

There have been many local drama and choral groups and they have given performances over the years, most of them in the Mission, or Alice Marshall, Hall.

1940s, a war-time production of 'A Little Learning'. Left to right: Nellie Cattle, —, George Laws, Eric Pratley, Joan Fleming.

'The Roaring Twenties' performed by the Choral Society in the 1960s. Left to right, back row: Nita and Peter Watts, Sarah Pratley, Deanna Gardner, Derek Gardner, Tony Smith. Front row: Dave Shirley, Pam Frost, —, Pauline Jarvis, Barbara Eddy.

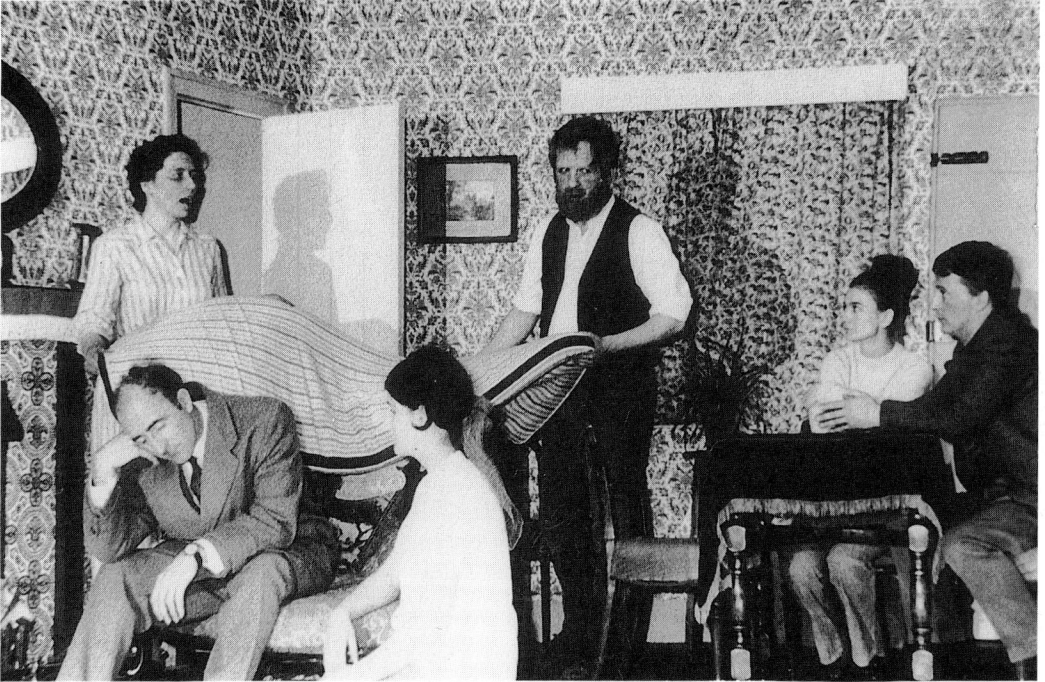

'Love in the Mist', 1971. Left to right, back: Joyce Morley, Peter Hicks, Sue Hough, Alan Lock. Front: John Cooper, Jenny Croft.

The Middle Barton Drama Group was formed in 1985 and has given performances each year since then with several pantomimes written by local actor/author Martin Roberts.

Left to right: Christine Outtridge, Martin Roberts, Michael Horwood-Smith and Karen Brown in 'Brush with a Body' in 1987. (*The Oxford Times*)

Middle Barton Ballet School was set up by Ann Gross in 1976, and seven pupils took exams two years later when they travelled to London in the snow and danced in a draughty hall. All were successful and, since then, many pupils have passed exams — no longer having to travel to London. Productions have been mounted though some performed elsewhere as the stage in the village is not large enough.

Sweet Dreams in 'Christmas is Love' in 1985. On the left, Coconut Ice. Left to right, back row: Catherine Woods, Kathryn Squire, Sarah Wilesmith. Front row: Elizabeth Aplin, Abigail Day, Karyn Chesterman. On the right, Liquorice Sticks. Carolyn and Sonya Gross, Melanie Woodley, Elizabeth Fay, Alyson Gross.

Barton Wives

They were called Young Wives in 1968 but the years passed, everyone became older, so the name was changed to Barton Wives Regular meetings are no longer held. This dinner dance, with husbands, was at Hopcroft's Holt Hotel in 1971. Left to right, facing the camera: Tessa and John Burt, Geoffrey and Ann Preston.

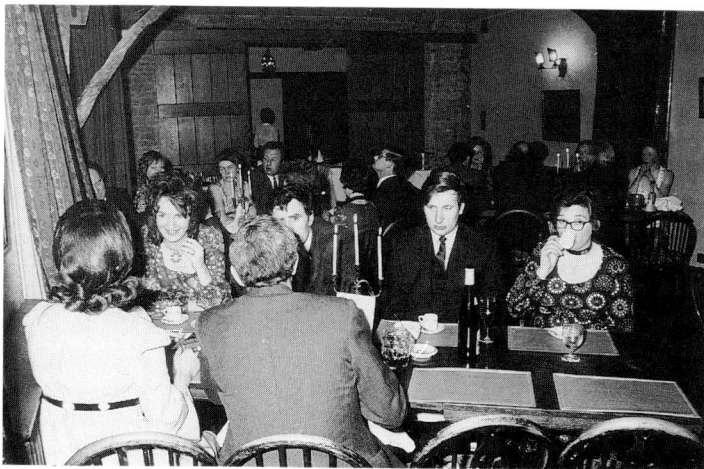

Bartons History Group

This informal group was set up in 1985 to collect and record information about The Bartons. Exhibitions have been held and some booklets published.

Village Information

A monthly news sheet *Bartons and Sandford Bulletin,* giving details of local activities and events, has been circulated to all households since 1970. It is financed by the Parish Councils and Parish Meeting in the area. A larger magazine, *The Dorn Free Press,* started in 1994 and, financed by advertising, is circulated every two months in the same area.

Farming and Families

This is far from being a complete record of either subject. The photographs and bill-heads are used in addition to those elsewhere in the book, to give an extra nostalgic glance at some aspects of a farming system, now greatly changed, and to some of the families who have lived here and some who have had businesses here.

Helping with the harvest c1950. Left to right: Cyril Shirley, Tony Moulder, Ernest Hawker of Sycamore Farm, John Bolton, Ron Gascoigne.

Milkman Tom Hope in the 1920s at Church Farm, then known as Goffe's Farm.

1920s. Frank Hazell and Jim Harper at Constable's farm in South Street.

Marjorie Smith, who later married Bill Irons, on his first tractor, bought in the 1930s.

Martha Matthews, c1905, with daughters Florence Annie and Nellie Florence.

Annie Hollis Stockford, c1917, with her children Tom, Rachel and William.

1925. Solomon and Eliza Stewart in the doorway with Edie, Sid, Doll, Bob. Seated: William, Muriel.

Emma Baker with daughters Lily and Violet c1910.

Village Events

Club Days, Flower Shows, Fetes, Choir and Sunday School outings used to be eagerly awaited events. Holidays were few and people made the most of them. Club Days were held annually by the Barton Friendly Society and were popular events.

These photographs were taken of the Club Day in 1909. The banner shows the date, 1858, when the Barton Friendly Society was founded.

The Friendly Society was set up to provide an insurance scheme to help with costs of burial and illness. When new social insurance measures were introduced, the Society, in 1915, became part of the Oxfordshire and United Counties Friendly Society. There was still a local collector, George H. Kirby, and in 1921 there were 101 men and 15 women members each contributing 11½d a week.

Club Day was an occasion that was much enjoyed, and the entry in the school log-book for July 20th in 1909 was: *'Barton Club Day, School closed.'*

The flower shows, too, were great events. Everyone wore their best clothes and absent members of the family all came to visit if they possibly could. Many photographs were taken by the indefatigable Frank Packer of Chipping Norton and these, as postcards, were sent to absent family and friends, often with an X marking the picture of a sender or a relation. Most of the flower shows were held either at the Rectory in Westcote Barton or at Barton Abbey, in Steeple Barton.

The judging of the produce was important and serious but when that was over there were races and sports and usually, in the evening, a dance.

1916. At the starting line with eggs and spoons: Left to right: −, Nellie Probbitts, Mona Kirby, Bertha Stockford, Rachel Stockford, Winnie Kirby, Sybil Stockford, Revd J E Cardigan-Williams, Vicar of Sandford St Martin.

1921. A good display of hats.

The organising of the events was a serious business.

The Committee in the 1920s. Left to right, back row: Percival Grimsley, Charles Marsh, Albert Paine, Charles Boffin, George Hopes, Ronnie Riach, Solomon Stewart, —, James Hurst, Pop Hopes. Middle row: William Brain, James Canty, George Stockford, George Brooks, Jethro Callow. Front row: Ben Stockford, — Boffin, though these two were not perhaps active members of the committee!

At that time the committee members were men and the refreshment team women. Left to right, back row: Agnes Austin, —, Frances Goffe, Polly Woolford. Front row: Flo Wheeler, Floss Jeffries, Ethel Paine, Eva Stickland, —.

Les Newman collected 'museum pieces' and his bicycles were on display at the 1951 Flower Show at the playing fields.

Les Newman with son Michael perched aloft, Ernest Allen, and Frederick Towsey were joined by Mick Buller from Heyford.

The 1961 Flower Show at the Rectory, Westcote Barton. (*Banbury Guardian*) Gwendolyn Wilmot Griffiths, Pat Groves, Susan Young. Children: Valerie Bassett, Sarah Pratley. Flower shows have been revived by the Bartons and District Horticultural Society. These are held at the Sports and Social Club and consist of classes for flowers and produce.

Fetes were also a great day out and were then, as now, money raising events. An item in the Woodstock Ruridecanal Magazine of September 1923 gave a colourful report of the recent fete. *'Over 1000 came. Charabancs came from a distance, as far as Oxford. The Sports on the lake organised by Mr Riach and Mr W Bennett jun were the principal attractions. Everyone swept down to watch. Mr Riach and Mr Bennett had elaborated a very ambitious plan of aquatic engineering which was admirably executed by Messrs Irons and Marsh and other willing assistants. A water shute towering 20ft high led to various mysterious devices cropping out of the water. There were swimming races and obstacle races involving the shute, tubes and poles. All arrangements were in place for water football but time failed. The Oxford Wireless Telephony Co Ltd broadcast programmes and the ring of the apparatus was so true to the natural voice that everyone wished they could have it in their homes.'*

By 1928 country dancing was popular and a team was photographed at a fete at Barton Abbey in 1928. Left to right, back row: , −, −, −, Mary Bayliss, Nurse Parrish, Mary Ostler. Middle row: Nellie Probbitts, Hilda Brain, −, Susan Howard, Edith Silver. Front row: Agatha Ayres, Doris Goffe, Mona Kirby, Ethel Paine. Some of the members who are not identified came from Steeple Aston.

Mona Kirby, when she had become Mona Owen, remembered some sixty years later that the dress she was wearing was green with white spots and was obtained from Swan & Edgar in London, having been ordered 'on appro', or on approval.

Punting on the lake at a flower show at Barton Abbey in 1916. The baby was Doris Baker, now Doris Bricknell.

Punting on the mill stream at a chapel fete in about 1930, not long before the mill was closed and the channel for the stream filled in. The house in the background of the picture is 16 South Street.

National Events

Steeple Barton

Her Majesty's Jubilee Celebration. June 23ʳᵈ 1887.

Amateur Athletic Sports.

For Amateurs Only !!

Among the national events celebrated was Queen Victoria's Golden Jubilee in 1887 when there were races and cricket matches at The Sands in Steeple Barton.

Elizabeth R
1953

THE BARTONS
Coronation Celebrations

Tuesday, June 2nd, 1953

Free TELEVISION at the Mission Hall
from 10.15 a.m. till 5.20 p.m.

Free television in 1953 was a great event and the hall was full to overflowing. Sports and matches took place at the playing fields and a dance in the evening was followed by fireworks.

The Bartons featured in a television programme in 1977. A Jubilee Queen, Jenny Charles, was chosen and a bonfire was lit at Steeple Barton. The decorated floats the following day were a highlight of the celebrations. Floats assembled in a field, which now has Holliers Crescent houses built on it, and processed along North Street for the Grand Parade and Judging at the Playing Fields. Nearly all the organisations in the village entered a float and the fire breathing entry of the United States Air Force at Upper Heyford base will long be remembered.

THE BARTONS JUBILEE CELEBRATIONS

1977

THE QUEEN'S SILVER JUBILEE

War Time

The Barton Home Guard's first volunteer enrolled in May 1940 and, between then and December 1944, 73 soldiers, under the command of Major Philip Fleming, served in the Platoon. The majority were just under military age or well above it.

Members of the Home Guard in 1941, on the bank outside what is now 1 North Street, soon after they had been issued with proper uniforms. Left to right, back row: Frank Gascoigne, Arthur Bosley, Tom Hazell, Tom Stewart, Charlie Davis, Archie Price, Hedley Gardiner, Alec Gardiner, Will West. Middle row: Derek Pritchard, Harry Bassett, John Butcher, Will Baker, Norman Cross, Philip Fleming, Harry Stevens, Ralph Greenslade, Charlie Eaglestone. Front row: Charlie Boffin, George (Pudgy) Simson, Bill Meakin, Arthur (Baggy) Wilkes, Jack Eaglestone, Charlie Hazell, Bunty Simson, Reg Shirley.

In 1941 the Home Guard and Civil Defence Services marched to Steeple Barton Church preceded by the Liverpool Irish pipe band. This photograph shows the parade passing the Duchess of Marlborough outside the barn of Church Farm.

Red Cross sewing groups made dressings for hospitals, when white overalls and head dresses had to be worn. This group was at work in Barton Abbey in 1941.

From front left, round the table: Winifred Probitts, Harriet Evans, Elsie Hope, 'Bubbles' Stockford, Hilarie Hope, Margaret Hawker, Gladys Lindsay, Hilda Dillon, — Williams, Winnie Gooding, Dorothy Durnford, Ada Stockford, Sarah —, Joan West, Alice Price, — Knight. Standing: Ellen? Churchill, Germaine —, Mildred West. Lady Dillon lived at Barton Lodge and several members of the group were on the staff at there.

Women also, through the Women's Institute, helped in many ways, particularly with evacuees and preservation of food. Others did munitions work at the aluminium factory in Banbury — those on the day shift remember catching the bus at 4.30 a.m.

Evacuees in 1941. These were older pupils from St Anthony's School in Forest Hill who went to school at Steeple Aston. The headteacher of St Anthony's, Mr Webster, and his wife are on the right and left of the photograph and Kathleen Saich in the centre. The picture brought back memories to Peggy Lombard as her brother married the sister of two of the children in the photograph.

The war time building in a field on The Bartons side of the main road near Hopcroft's Holt, is a reminder of the time when aircraft were kept in that field and it is believed that bombs which dropped along both sides of the main road one Thursday afternoon, were aimed at those planes.

There was little enemy action here but one evening a Wellington bomber crashed in a field near Whistlow. Peggy, daughter of Thomas and Alice Gascoigne, who was in the Women's Royal Air Force and home on leave, is remembered as helping to rescue the rear gunner. The other members of the crew were killed.

Air Raid Precautions and National Fire Service

The ARP and NFS were active during war time. Charles Ayres, former headteacher of the village school, was Warden in charge of the ARP and meetings were held in the billiard room at his house, 47 North Street. Bert Cross and Bill Courtnell helped him. Charlie Gibbons and Bob Jarvis were in charge of the NFS and were helped by, among others, Bill Matthews and Fred Carpenter.

St John Ambulance Brigade Barton Division

The Barton Division was formed in 1939 after a training course with sessions every week over a period of three months. Thirtynine people finished the course out of the 45 who started. Members of the Division worked closely with all the groups engaged in war-time activities.

It was organised by Reginald Stickland from the Medical Comforts Depot at his house in Fox Lane (No. 6). By 1945 the Division had an ambulance and this picture was taken at Barton Abbey in the late 1940s.

The Ambulance Service continued after the war. There was a team of St John Ambulance nurses and eight voluntary drivers. The service covered the surrounding villages and was used two or three times a week.

A report on their work in 1948 was given in the February 1949 issue of the Woodstock Ruridecanal Magazine: *'57 invalids conveyed, 5 road accidents, 14 house accidents'.*

IN MEMORY OF THOSE WHO GAVE
THEIR LIVES IN TWO WORLD WARS

1914 — 1918

Harold (Bidmead) Bassett
Frederick Carpenter
Horace Vaughan Castle
William John Clack
Frederick William Constable
John Constable
Ernest James Hawkins
Ernest James Hawkins
Albert Edward Hawkins
George Henry Hawkins
William Edward Humphries
William Keen
George Felix Kirby
Frederick John Luing
Jenner Stephen Chance Marshall
William James Parsons
William W Proffitt
Nigel Stewart Riach
John Edwin Smith
Charles Steven
Horace Percy Stewart
Felix Francis George Stockford
Walter Allison Woodruff

1939 — 1945

Walter Henry Boffin
Frederick John Shirley

They are commemorated in the parish churches and a Book of Remembrance is kept at the Sports and Social Club at the playing fields, the playing fields which were created as a memorial after the Second World War.